A QUICK GUIDE TO
BEHAVIOUR
MANAGEMENT

PACKED FULL OF
PRACTICAL ADVICE,
EXAMPLES, QUICK
TIPS, AND HANDY
SOLUTIONS

BOB BATES
ANDY BAILEY
DEREK LEVER

A QUICK GUIDE TO
BEHAVIOUR
MANAGEMENT

$SAGE

Los Angeles | London | New Delhi
Singapore | Washington DC | Melbourne

$SAGE

Los Angeles | London | New Delhi
Singapore | Washington DC | Melbourne

SAGE Publications Ltd
1 Oliver's Yard
55 City Road
London EC1Y 1SP

SAGE Publications Inc.
2455 Teller Road
Thousand Oaks, California 91320

SAGE Publications India Pvt Ltd
B 1/I 1 Mohan Cooperative Industrial Area
Mathura Road
New Delhi 110 044

SAGE Publications Asia-Pacific Pte Ltd
3 Church Street
#10-04 Samsung Hub
Singapore 049483

Editor: Delayna Spencer
Editorial assistant: Orsod Malik
Production editor: Nicola Carrier
Copyeditor: Sharon Cawood
Proofreader: Samantha Lacey
Indexer: Gary Kirby
Marketing manager: Dilhara Attygalle
Cover design: Wendy Scott
Typeset by: C&M Digitals (P) Ltd, Chennai, India
Printed in the UK

© Bob Bates, Andy Bailey & Derek Lever, 2019

First published 2019

Library of Congress Control Number: 2018961595

British Library Cataloguing in Publication data

A catalogue record for this book is available from
the British Library

ISBN 978-1-5264-2464-8
ISBN 978-1-5264-2465-5 (pbk)

At SAGE we take sustainability seriously. Most of our products are printed in the UK using responsibly sourced
papers and boards. When we print overseas we ensure sustainable papers are used as measured by the PREPS
grading system. We undertake an annual audit to monitor our sustainability.

CONTENTS

LIST OF FIGURES AND APPENDICES

FIGURES

APPENDICES

ABOUT THE AUTHORS

Amongst the writers of this book there is well over a hundred years' experience of working with learners from primary through to post-compulsory education, many of whom displayed challenging behaviour. Do we know all of the answers to dealing with them? Of course not! We can only share with you our thoughts on this issue and leave it you to decide what approaches you can adapt and adopt to suit the challenges that you face.

Bob Bates is an adult education teacher educator. He has a PhD in education and has taught over 1000 teachers on graduate and post-graduate programmes at two universities and in adult education centres. Bob has taught behaviour management classes on a number of these programmes and to major national private training providers such as the Rathbone Society.

This is Bob's sixth book. *The Little Book of BIG Management Theories*, written with Jim McGrath and published by Pearson in 2014, was on WHSmith's bestsellers list for 9 months and is being translated into 17 languages. His first solo book, *The Little Book of Big Coaching Models*, published by Pearson in 2015, was also a bestseller and was described by Sir Dave Brailsford (Team Sky cycling director) as a 'great read'. It is currently being translated into German and Thai. His third book, *Learning Theories Simplified*, was published by SAGE in the autumn of 2015 (the second edition was published in 2019). His fourth book, *A Quick Guide to Special Educational Needs and Disabilities*, was published by SAGE in 2016. His fifth book, *Leadership Theories Simplified*, written with Andy Bailey, was published by SAGE in 2017.

Andy Bailey has been an education practitioner for nearly 50 years. He was the head teacher of a primary school in the West Midlands for 26 years from 1983 until 2009. From 2000 until 2005 he was an external advisor for the National Programme for the Performance Management of Head Teachers. He was a School Improvement Partner, employed by the Birmingham and Walsall Education Authorities to work with a number of schools between 2006 and 2011. From 2012 until 2015 he was an inspector for Ofsted working as a lead inspector in 2014 and 2015. Since his retirement from his head teacher's post, he has worked as a consultant in a number of primary schools in Birmingham and Walsall.

Andy has also written or co-written a number of educational publications for practitioners and pupils in England and Wales and the Caribbean and has lectured to teachers, managers and advisors in a number of local authorities and universities in England and the Caribbean.

Derek Lever has been a practitioner in education for over 50 years. He has taught pupils from 4 to 16 years of age, was an acting head teacher in three rural primary schools in the 1970s and head teacher of two large, urban primary schools from 1980 to 1993. He has run head teacher training programmes and also spent 12 months as head of a learning and resource centre. He has been an external examiner and an associate lecturer at two universities. In 1993, he was appointed as Walsall MBC's schools' inspector for mathematics 4–18 and subsequently a general school's inspector, before becoming Deputy to the Chief Education Officer in 1997. For six years, he was an Inspector for Ofsted and helped establish a Consortium of local education authorities who conducted inspections and trained inspectors on behalf of Ofsted.

He has Bachelor and Master's degrees in education and added the award of Doctorate at Loughborough University in the 1990s. In collaboration with university colleagues, he has had a range of articles published and a book, *What do Primary School Headteachers Really Do?* (a LUDEO publication in 1997). He has spoken at international conferences in various parts of the world, including Austria, Denmark, Romania, Portugal and the USA and also arranged and conducted study visits for colleagues in and from several countries, including Malawi, France and New Zealand. In 2011, he was contracted by a prominent UK company to collaborate on a review of the New York City school effectiveness programme.

INTRODUCTION

Read through the following scenarios and see which one applies to you the most:

- **Scenario A**: You feel completely relaxed and comfortable during lessons and able to undertake any form of lesson activity without concern. Classroom control is not really an issue as you and your learners are working together, enjoying the experiences involved. You are completely in control of the class but may need to exercise some authority at times to maintain a calm and purposeful working atmosphere. This is done in a friendly and relaxed manner and is no more than a gentle reminder to your learners. **You believe that teaching is a great profession**.
- **Scenario B**: You feel tense and anxious during lessons. Classroom control is non-existent. The use of resources is largely ignored by learners. When you write on the whiteboard, items are being thrown around. You go into the room hoping they will chat to each other and leave you alone. Sometimes your entry into the classroom is greeted by derision and abuse. There are so many rules being broken that you feel it is difficult to know where to start. You start to turn a blind eye to appalling behaviour because you are afraid that any intervention could lead to confrontation or escalation of the problem. **You wish you hadn't gone into teaching**.

If it's always Scenario A, we're wondering why you bought this book. If it's always Scenario B, we suspect that you may need to do some serious thinking about your future in teaching. The likelihood is that you will flit between these two extremes depending on how both you and your learners are feeling on a particular day.

Sue Cowley, writer of the much acclaimed *Getting the Buggers to Behave* book, claims that, with a well-behaved class, teaching is one of the most wonderful jobs in the world. We don't dispute this. This book however is more about dealing with the other end of the spectrum and what Donald Schön, in *The Reflective Practitioner*, refers to as the swampy lowland masses that occur in classrooms when learners' challenging behaviour is preventing learning from taking place and teaching is becoming a misery.

The 2016 Bennett report, *Developing Behaviour Management Content for Initial Teacher Training*, stresses the importance of having structured classroom routines, strategies and interventions for de-escalating confrontation and resolving conflict and regulating one's own emotional state by understanding personal triggers in one's own behaviour, expectations or reactions. Bennett makes the point that 'managing behaviour is best learned by doing, by making those mistakes all teachers make early in their careers and having the opportunity to reflect on those mistakes and get back in the classroom to try again as soon as possible'.

We wanted to provide trainee teachers, newly qualified teachers and experienced teachers with some information as to what may be causing the more extreme challenging behaviour, and some practical tips on how to support learners when this happens. Although it's the pragmatic approach that Bennett advocates, and will appeal to most people who want a quick reference guide, we didn't want to dispense with some interesting theories that underpin the suggested approaches. We have tried therefore to blend an understanding of learning theories with the experiences of a number of teachers and trainers, at various stages in their careers, who had to deal with challenging behaviours.

We don't advocate for one minute that this book will be a remedy for all of the problems you are facing or likely to face in the classroom, but it will help you to understand challenging behaviour and to be able to develop strategies for coping with some of the more challenging behaviour that you will encounter.

The book is divided into three parts:

Part 1 deals with the What? Why? Who? It sets the scene for Parts B and C and includes definitions, theories and models of good practice in understanding more about the causes of challenging behaviour. This part also addresses some of the myths surrounding behaviour management that reflect popular opinion about what many perceive to be the fundamental principles of effective behaviour management. Like any use of theories and models in education, the ones used throughout the book range from the pedagogical to the psychological.

Part 2 deals with the How? It offers practical advice on how to be a great teacher in the face of challenging behaviour. This part discusses the rights that you have as a teacher, the importance of knowing what your default position is and how to plan your teaching strategies. It also covers three important issues facing educationalists (special needs, victims of abuse and radicalisation) that will almost certainly have an impact on learners' behaviour. Part B concludes with some advice on how to deal with the stress that you will face when dealing with challenging behaviour.

Part 3 deals with a range of characters displaying challenging behaviours that you may face in the classroom, and strategies for dealing with them. The use of examples is an essential feature of this part of the book. The examples are mostly drawn from real incidents that occurred in the classroom, with occasional references to fictional accounts, and serve to indicate the impact of that type of behaviour on teachers and others in the classroom.

Please note that throughout the book we use the terms:

- 'organisation' to cover schools, colleges, universities and training providers
- 'teacher' to cover anyone involved in the teaching/training process
- 'learner' to apply to whoever it is that is being taught or trained
- 'classroom' to describe the setting where teaching/training is taking place
- 'lesson' to describe the teaching/training activity.

The principles and practices covered in the book are relevant whether you are: (a) working with children, young people or adults; or (b) a teacher, trainer, coach or mentor.

PART 1

INTRODUCTION

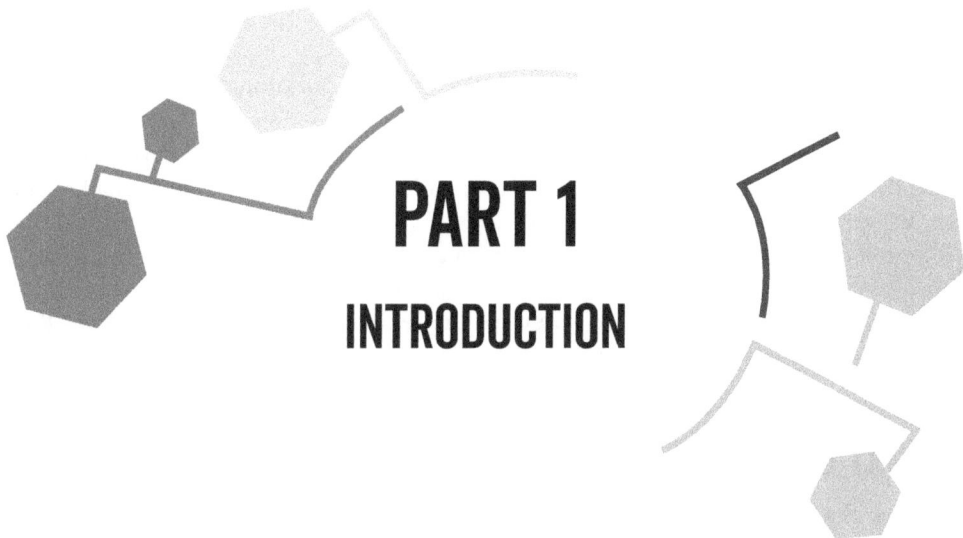

In this part of the book, we want to discuss what we mean by challenging behaviour, why it occurs and who's to blame. In doing this, we challenge some of the commonly held assumptions about behaviour and some of the myths that have grown up around this.

1.1 WHAT IS CHALLENGING BEHAVIOUR?

It's important that we qualify here what we mean by challenging behaviour. As a teacher, this doesn't just mean dealing with violent or offensive behaviour; it's any behaviour that disrupts normal classroom routine and the concentration of other learners. For the purposes of this book, we have grouped and refer to the different types of challenging behaviour, as either:

- **Intimidatory** behaviour: behaviour that is aggressive, offensive or violent towards others. This includes physical and psychological intimidation or verbal abuse.
- **Inappropriate** behaviour: behaviour that is more annoying than intimidatory, but is of such a persistent and prolific nature that it disrupts classroom routine.
- **Non-participative** behaviour: behaviour that is extremely passive or non-engaging, including refusal to participate in activities or intermittent patterns of attendance.

- **Demanding** behaviour: behaviour that is driven by the learner's self-interest and conscious or sub-conscious desires to want to dominate what takes place in the classroom.

These definitions are fairly broad and issues of special educational needs and disabilities may dictate what is considered to be challenging or acceptable behaviour in the classroom. In this respect, individual organisations need to define what they consider to be behaviour that is challenging but acceptable, and behaviour that is challenging but disruptive to staff and other learners. It's quite likely that even within the same institution there may be differences in individual teachers' perspectives on the subject. A useful exercise, in this respect, is to look at the scenarios covered in Part C and discuss with colleagues what their view of the learner's behaviour is and how they would have handled the situation.

1.2 WHY DOES IT HAPPEN?

Theories relating to understanding why people behave in the way they do date as far back as 500 BC and the Greek philosophers Plato and Aristotle. Plato argued that people had an intrinsic desire to do what they do, whereas Aristotle's view was that it is something that happens as a result of nurturing. The *nature vs nurture* debate is one of the oldest issues in human development that focuses on the relative contributions of genetic inheritance and environmental conditioning.

For many years, this was a philosophical debate with well-known thinkers such as René Descartes suggesting that certain behaviours are inherent in people, or that they simply occur naturally (the *nativist* viewpoint), arguing the toss with others such as John Locke who believed in the principle of *tabula rasa*, which suggests the mind begins as a blank slate and that our behaviours are determined by our experiences (the *empiricist* viewpoint). Towards the end of the 19th century, the debate was taken up by a new breed of theorists who developed the discipline of psychology.

For most of the early part of the 20th century, behavioural psychologists, such as Watson, Skinner and Pavlov, suggested that humans were simply advanced mammals that reacted to stimuli. *Behaviourism* remained the basis of human conditioning until it was challenged in the period between the two world wars by psychologists, such as Piaget and Vygotsky, who argued that the way we behave is a cognitive process in which individuals shape their own reaction to a situation rather than being told what to do. This gave rise to the movement known as *cognitivism*. After the Second World War, a third branch of theory, championed by people such as Maslow and Rogers, came into force with the belief that people were individuals whose behaviour should not be separate from life itself and who should be given the opportunity to determine for themselves the nature of their own actions. This became known as *humanism*.

The new millennium, and the growing interest in neuroscience, provided a fresh insight into how people react through their capacity to process external stimuli. Although theories around what role the brain plays in this process are still mostly speculative, there does appear to be common consent that the mind was set up to process external stimuli, to draw connections with other stimuli and, by making sense of what is happening, behave in what they consider to be an appropriate manner.

Few people these days would take such an extreme position in this debate as to argue for one side at the absolute exclusion of the other. There are just too many factors on both sides of the argument which would deter an all-or-nothing view. Figure 1.1 is a snapshot of the range of theories relating to this subject.

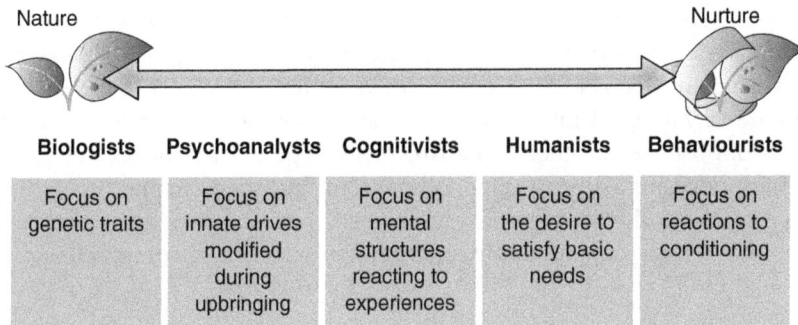

Nature				Nurture
Biologists	**Psychoanalysts**	**Cognitivists**	**Humanists**	**Behaviourists**
Focus on genetic traits	Focus on innate drives modified during upbringing	Focus on mental structures reacting to experiences	Focus on the desire to satisfy basic needs	Focus on reactions to conditioning

Figure 1.1   The nature–nurture theoretical spectrum

Here are some guidelines to determine where you might have a tendency towards in this debate:

- If you are at the extreme end of the Nature scale, the likelihood is that you will believe that the genetic structure of an individual's brain is mostly responsible for their behaviour.
- As you start to move towards the centre of the scale, you begin to accept the viewpoint that the genetic structure of the brain is capable of being modified in response to reactions to experiences and the environment and that it is this that determines how people behave.
- Moving from the centre towards the end of the Nurture scale, you are likely to favour the ideas of the humanist theorists and the significance they attach to society's influence on an individual's behaviour.
- At the extreme end of the Nurture scale, the likelihood is that you will believe in the arguments of the behaviourists who suggest that all behaviour can be modified through conditioning.

There is no neat and simple way of resolving this debate. The more you read on the subject, the more confusing it gets. The best advice we can give is to go with what feels right for you. You could also try the exercise in Appendix 2 for some thoughts on this.

1.3 WHO'S TO BLAME?

We'd like to pause at this stage and ask you to reflect on where you consider the blame for disruptive behaviour lies. If you have an extreme *naturist* view, you will believe that learners have a disruptive behavioural gene. If however you are an extreme *nurturist*, then you will accept that learners' reactions to the behaviour of others, including their teachers, influences their disruptive behaviour. Now, there's an interesting suggestion: that learners' disruptive behaviour could be as much a result of your actions as it is of theirs.

During our behaviour management sessions with trainee teachers, we do an exercise involving two cans of fizzy pop and lots of cleaning towels. We ask for four volunteers. Two are stooges who we have briefed what to do prior to the session. The other two are unwitting victims. The victims are given cleaning towels and asked to sit in chairs opposite each other about two metres apart. The stooges are each given a can of fizzy pop and asked to stand behind their intended victims.

We then read out the scenario in example 1.1, pausing after each extract for the stooges to shake their cans as the frustration that each of the central characters feel starts to build up.

Example 1.1: The story of two lives on a wet Monday morning in February

A: Christine Adams is a 35-year-old teacher on the BTEC sports course at a local college. She was a B International Hockey player until she had to give up playing to look after her 7-year-old daughter, Amber, who has Down syndrome. She is a single parent. She gets up at 7:00am to make a cup of coffee and finds there is no milk (SHAKE).

B: Joey Campbell is a 16-year-old student in Christine's class. He was a former soccer trainee with the Derby Football School of Excellence and a promising prospect until a ligament injury ended his career. He lives with his mum and two younger sisters. His mother works as a cleaner at a local school. He has to get his sisters to school in the morning, He has to be awake at 7:00am. Desperate for a cigarette, he finds an empty packet (SHAKE).

A: Christine's childminder calls to say she has a rash and can't look after Amber today (SHAKE).

B: Joey's younger sister can't find her shoes and starts crying (SHAKE).

A: Christine dashes round to her mother-in-law's house to see if she can look after Amber. Reluctantly, the mother-in-law agrees but has a go at Christine for being a bad mother (SHAKE).

B: As they get near to the school, Joey's older sister tells him she has forgotten her gym kit. Joey has to run back to get it (SHAKE).

A: Christine gets into class five minutes before the start of the lesson (SHAKE).

B: Joey gets into class ten minutes after the start of the lesson (SHAKE).

A: Christine asks Joey why he was late (SHAKE).

B: Joey starts to explain (SHAKE).

A: Christine says 'excuses, excuses' (SHAKE).

B: Joey tries again to explain (SHAKE).

A: Christine cuts him off (SHAKE vigorously).

B: Joey storms out of the class (SHAKE vigorously).

At this point, we ask both of the *stooges* to 'point the can of fizzy pop at their victims and on the count of three to open the can'. We've had people close their eyes at this stage, someone once screamed and someone even jumped out of the chair. Obviously, the *stooges* are briefed not to open the can. We're sure that one day one of us will forget to brief them properly and be faced with a hefty cleaning bill.

The point of this exercise is to show that friction between teacher and learner in the classroom can arise as a result of the emotional state of either party. We ask the group to stay with the fizzy pop analogy and say how they can prevent their victims getting covered with pop. We usually get the following responses: Don't shake the can so vigorously, leave the pop to settle down, get rid of the can or open it very slowly.

We then get them to come back to the scenario and discuss how Christine could have handled the situation better. We usually get that she could have:

• relaxed and listened to what Joey had to say
• explained that she'd had a bad start to the day and that they wipe the slate clean and start again
• postponed dealing with Joey till the end of the lesson when things may have cooled down
• stayed in bed.

If there is one common thread running throughout the dealings with all of the challenging characters included in Part C, it's about understanding what the cause of their behaviour is and reacting appropriately to this. Showing that you are angry with someone isn't always a good course of action but not necessarily always the wrong approach. Aristotle wrote that 'anybody can become angry – that is easy, but to be angry with the right person, to the right degree, at the right time, for the right purpose and in the right way is not within everybody's power and is not easy'. Get any one of these wrong and you could cause long-term damage to your relationship with the individual or, worse, be facing disciplinary action for harassment.

1.4 THE MYTHS OF BEHAVIOUR MANAGEMENT

Never displaying anger towards a challenging individual is one of the myths that have grown up around the teaching profession. Aristotle says that it is okay to be angry with the right person at the right time for the right reason. Here are some other myths that we'd like to debunk:

MYTH #1: TEACHING IS A VIRTUE OF CHARACTER NOT INTELLECT

No, you haven't misread this. We are challenging Aristotle's view of teaching and claiming that only intelligent teachers can be in control of the challenging children in their class. We need to qualify what we mean here.

Intellect has for many years been measured using Intelligence Quotient (IQ) tests. In more recent years, these tests have been criticised for failing to take account of the complex nature of the human intellect and the inference that there are links between intellectual ability and characteristics such as race, gender and social class.

In this section, we want to look at the theories of two writers who offered different perspectives on the subject of intelligence: Howard Gardner, who introduced the concept of *multiple intelligences* (1993) and Daniel Goleman, who introduced the concept of *emotional intelligence* (1996).

Howard Gardner (1993) proposed that human beings have several types of intelligence that form the potential to process information in a range of different contexts and cultures. His nine intelligences are:

- **Linguistic**: the capacity to understand and use spoken and written language.
- **Logical–Mathematical**: the capacity to analyse problems logically.
- **Bodily–Kinaesthetic**: the capacity to use and interpret expressive movement.
- **Visual–Spatial**: the capacity to recognise patterns and dimensions.
- **Musical**: the capacity to compose, perform and appreciate musical patterns.
- **Interpersonal**: the capacity to understand the intentions and desires of others.
- **Intrapersonal**: the capacity to understand one's own feelings, fears and needs.
- **Naturalistic**: the capacity to recognise and categorise objects in nature.
- **Spiritualistic**: the capacity to tackle deep questions about the meaning of life.

Gardner made two fundamental claims about his ideas: first, that they accounted for the full range of human cognition; and, second, that each individual has a unique blend of the various intelligences that has made them who they are. Identifying individual differences amongst a group of individuals in your class will help you to be better at understanding the learning process and more prepared to work with all learners. Failure to do this can lead to frustration on the part of the learner which in turn can result in them disrupting the class.

Daniel Goleman (1996) suggested that intelligence is not just about developing a high IQ or being technically skilled, but that people also need to develop their emotional intelligence. He argued that there are five key elements of emotional intelligence, which we have interpreted for teachers. These are summarised as:

- **Self-awareness**: teachers must be aware of the relationship between their thoughts, feelings and actions. They must be able to recognise what thoughts about a situation sparked off which emotions and the impact these emotions can have on themselves and those around them.
- **Managing emotions**: teachers must analyse what is behind these emotions and be able to deal with them in a positive manner.
- **Empathy**: teachers must be able to deal with the emotions of those in their class in a positive manner. This requires them to be able to understand more about the nature of any concerns being expressed about their teaching.
- **Social skills**: teachers need to develop quality relationships. This will have a positive effect on all involved. Knowing how and when to take the lead and when to follow is an essential social skill.
- **Motivation**: teachers can't always rely on external rewards to motivate others. They must support their learners to develop their own source of intrinsic motivators by encouraging them to appreciate what they can do and not to focus on the things they can't do.

Goleman argued that having a high level of self-awareness and an understanding of others makes you a better person as well as a better teacher.

You may have read somewhere that we're born with a huge amount of brain cells but lose thousands every day till we die. That's the bad news. The good news is that neuroscientists claim that, rather than losing cells, the brain continuously reshapes itself in line with the experiences we have. Goleman claims that by persisting with positive thoughts and actions your newly reformed brain will ensure you will have a positive outlook in how you work as a teacher and will result in you naturally doing the right thing for your learners, in the right way. Of course, this is Goleman's theory, but doesn't it sound good and worth trying out? If you agree then here are some tips to help you:

- Develop your self-awareness by keeping a record of any disruptive incidents that take place in the classroom. A simple note of what happened, why it happened, what you did and what impact it had on you and those around you will suffice.
- Try to look at the situation from the learners' perspectives. Although you may disagree with their behaviour, recognising what's causing it will make you more capable of dealing with the situation.
- Listen carefully to what learners have to say and never be afraid to re-examine your own values in light of this.
- Always try to find a win–win solution to any situation arising with you and your learners.

Although they have a popular following, critics of both Goleman and Gardner claim that they can only speculate that their theories on intelligence are any more valid than the reliance on IQ testing.

> **Hot Tip:** Acting aggressively or passively may get you results in the short term but always trying for a win-win resolution when dealing with challenging behaviour will work better in the long term.

MYTH #2: 'POWER TENDS TO CORRUPT ... AND ABSOLUTE POWER CORRUPTS ABSOLUTELY'

This is a quote attributed to John Dalberg-Acton, a historian, politician and writer in the mid-19th century. Dalberg-Acton went on to say that 'great men are almost always bad men'. Of course, history is riddled with people who have abused the power or authority that they have been given or taken. Before we accept or reject this myth, we need to understand what we mean by power. There are numerous models of power. One of the most compelling was outlined by the sociologist Max Weber.

Weber (2002) identified three sources of authority or power. In respect of teaching, these are:

- **Traditional**: where the legitimacy of the teacher's authority comes from tradition or custom. It is accepted by learners, or at least not challenged by them.
- **Legal**: where a teacher exerts power by virtue of the office that they hold. It is the authority that demands obedience to the office rather than the office holder.
- **Charismatic**: where authority grows out of the personal charm or the personality of the teacher. Weber distinguished it from the other forms of authority by claiming that learners do not accept the authority of the teacher by virtue of tradition or statute, but because they trust and believe in them.

Typically, a significant amount of legal power will come with the teacher's role. Most teachers will have little or no traditional power and some will probably have a degree of charismatic power. Teachers need to test the limits of each of these and, in the face of adverse teaching conditions, work to accumulate as many sources of power as possible.

It's not the nature of power that corrupts therefore, even if this power is absolute, but the people who wield it. Both Hitler and Martin Luther King had a powerful hold over their followers; one used it for violent purposes, the other to promote peaceful demonstrations. It is worth remembering, however, that both were chosen as the *Times Magazine* Men of the Year (Hitler in 1938 and Luther King in 1963).

Examples 1.2 and 1.3 are both cases of college leaders who exercised the power they held in different ways.

Example 1.2: Beware of new brooms

Mary was a surprise choice to be the principal of a new community-based college formed out of the merger of two adult education centres that delivered vocational training throughout a network of community centres in the borough. She had ousted the incumbent principals of the two centres, who became her vice-principals. Many were impressed by Mary's talk of her vision for the new college and the values of openness and trust that she wanted to underpin the vision. She won everyone over with her charisma. In the space of three years, she took the college from an adequate institution to an outstanding one. But there was a price to pay for this. In a document that she marked 'confidential – for management only', she wrote about her desire to take education provision away from community centres and into libraries. This would mean significant job losses and inconvenience for community-based learners who would have to travel further to attend classes. Staff morale was at an all-time low with five cases of harassment being waged against her. Sickness due to stress was quadrupled.

Mary left after three years as principal, during which time no member of the original, nine-strong senior management team was still in post, seven out of the original ten community centres that delivered training had closed down and funding for community-based vocational training was reduced to less than a quarter of its previous level.

Example 1.3: If it ain't broke, why fix it?

Tom was the principal of a large FE college. He had worked his way up from an engineering instructor through to the principal's post. He was generally looked on as a bit of a pragmatist whose philosophy was, 'if it works, it's good'. He had a knack of finding resources to fund even the most outrageous ideas if he thought it would benefit his staff or learners. This never endeared him to inspectors, with the college never scoring highly for Leadership and Management and overall grades never better than good. He was however widely respected by staff and most people who came into contact with him. On one occasion, concerned that staff had nowhere to have a break from students, Tom gave up his office to them as a staff room.

(Continued)

(Continued)

When he was asked where he would sit, he replied, 'In the classrooms or the canteen, anywhere where I can get the low-down on how we are doing and I don't get pestered every minute with phone calls and emails. If they want me, they'll find me'. There was never a title to describe his leadership style and we doubt whether he would have thanked anyone who gave him one.

Tom retired after 20 years in the same college. The college ratings flitted between adequate and good (never inadequate or outstanding) and the college merged with another to form one of the country's largest further education colleges.

It's difficult to weigh up here whether power was being used for the good of all or in the interests of the individual wielding it. Mary's intention was always to leave after three years, having taken the college to an outstanding grade. She achieved this, but at a price. On visiting the college regularly, it's distressing to hear what people there are saying about morale and their concerns for the future of the college. Tom's college no longer exists as a separate entity but, even after 15 years, he is still talked about with respect and affection.

Hot Tip: Know what sources of power you have access to as a teacher. Decide whether you are using them in a positive or negative manner. Identify who in your organisation exercises power and what can you learn from them.

MYTH #3: THE END DOESN'T JUSTIFY THE MEANS

The end justifying the means is a saying attributed to Niccolò Machiavelli. Machiavelli was a 16th-century Italian writer, who, out of work and looking for a job, wrote a job application to the Magnificent Lorenzo de Medici. In the history of the world, it was one of the longest job applications and was later published as *The Prince* (2004).

The Prince has been described by many as an amoral guide to behaviour and the term Machiavellian as being something that is characterised by deception and ruthlessness. Never one to avoid controversy, we are going to tease out a few extracts from *The Prince* that we hope will show Machiavelli in a different light. Although Machiavelli wrote the extracts with leaders in mind, we have interpreted them from a teaching perspective (please excuse the political incorrectness in the extracts – they were written in the 16th century):

- **'There is no other way to guard yourself against flattery than by making men understand that telling you the truth will not offend you.'** Don't encourage the sycophants in your class. Surround yourself with learners who are not self-serving and who will voice their opinions honestly and challenge you.
- **'Acknowledge the possibilities for failure: a skilful leader does better to act boldly than to try to guard against every possible eventuality.'** Encourage your learners never to be afraid of failure. Most learners will react badly when they fail at something, which often results in disruptive behaviour. Tell them that 'only those who do nothing never fail'.
- **'Without an opportunity, their abilities would have been wasted, and without their abilities, the opportunity would have arisen in vain.'** Make sure the learners in your class are allowed every opportunity to develop themselves both in terms of their attitudes to others as well as academically.
- **'All courses of action are risky, so prudence is not in avoiding danger but calculating risk and acting decisively.'** Encourage the learners in your class never to be afraid to take calculated risks. Tell them that the future is not set but they can help shape it by their willingness to take risks and act with conviction.
- **'It must be considered that there is nothing more difficult to carry out, nor more doubtful of success, nor more dangerous to handle, than to initiate a new order of things.'** Never abuse the power that you have in your role as teacher but accept that there will be occasions when you need to act in a ruthless manner in the interest of your school or your class.
- **'Minds are of three kinds: one is capable of thinking for itself; another is able to understand the thinking of others; and a third can neither think for itself nor understand the thinking of others. The first is of the highest excellence, the second is excellent, and the third is worthless.'** Many educational organisations are bogged down with performance figures and have little time for a feeling of belonging, status or worth. Their contract with you is based on a performance-related transaction and if they need to let you go, they will. Recognise this and you will never be disappointed or surprised by how you are treated when you are reprimanded for placing more emphasis on the personal development of your learners than on their performance on tests.

You are not the only Machiavellian in the world. They are evident in education policy makers, the head teachers in your organisation, the staff, the parents and even the learners in your class. If need be, protect yourself against others who believe that the ends justify the means. They are unlikely to shy away from causing you problems if it suits their purpose. Remember, it's better to be useful to another Machiavellian than to be their friend.

Hot Tip: We are not advocating that you should always be deceitful or ruthless as a teacher, but you should be able to play the game in the best interests of your organisation and its learners.

MYTH #4: TEACHERS NEED TO SET AN EXEMPLAR MODEL FOR GOOD BEHAVIOUR

Whilst there is little doubt that teachers should be a good role model, it's important to recognise that, like everyone else, teachers aren't infallible. If they were, they wouldn't be human. See what you think about example 1.4.

Example 1.4: A testing dilemma

Malcolm was a graphic designer on a post-graduate teacher training course. Bob was his tutor and had been made aware that just prior to starting the course, Malcolm's sister had died. Malcolm was always first in the class and eager to discuss things that Bob had covered in the previous session. He was also last out, often accompanying Bob to his car and discussing things that were covered in that session. His enthusiasm was infectious but his written work was a disaster.

The day before Malcolm's mid-term tutorial, Bob received an email from the head of department telling him that Malcolm's brother had been stabbed and killed in a gang fight. Imagine his surprise when Malcolm turned up for his tutorial. He told Bob that training to be a teacher was more than just a career move for him; it was his way to stay out of the gang culture.

Bob observed Malcolm teach on three occasions over the next term. Bob felt that he wasn't a bad teacher, relying more on enthusiasm than a precise appreciation of the subject. The problem was that his written work was dreadful and without Bob rewriting large chunks of his assignments, Malcolm was going to fail the course.

If you are working with someone like Malcolm, what would you do? Here's the dilemma that his tutor faced: If he chose to rewrite his assignments, was he being a good role model and setting a good example for him as a teacher? Ethically, he had a responsibility to the other trainees that he was teaching and to the standards of the profession. If he chose to rewrite his assignments, was he allowing the emotions of the situation to influence his actions? What impact was this likely to have on the way that Malcolm works with his learners? These are questions that he has been asking himself for the past 15 years. He doubts whether Malcolm will forget him, but maybe not for the right reasons. Being a good role model is a massive responsibility!

Albert Bandura (1977) based his theory of role modelling on controlled experiments conducted with two groups of children. One group of children witnessed scenes of adults physically and verbally attacking an inflatable doll. The other group witnessed scenes of adults caressing and talking affectionately to the doll. When the children were left alone with the doll, they automatically imitated the behaviour of the adults that they had observed.

Bandura suggests that the observational process is underpinned by the notion that behaviour modification is achieved by: observing the actions of others, mentally rehearsing whether these actions are appropriate and then initiating behaviour that was considered appropriate. In order for someone to successfully imitate the behaviour of a role model, Bandura suggested that the individual must:

- be encouraged to pay attention to the behaviour
- remember what was seen or heard
- have the capacity to reproduce the behaviour
- have the motivation to want to reproduce it.

He argued that people would be more receptive to modelling good behaviour if they believed that they were capable of executing the behaviour. He used the term *self-efficacy* to describe this.

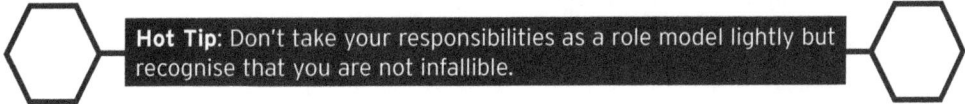

> **Hot Tip:** Don't take your responsibilities as a role model lightly but recognise that you are not infallible.

MYTH #5: IT WAS EASIER TO CONTROL LEARNERS IN THE 1950S AND 1960S WHEN DISCIPLINE WAS MUCH FIRMER

The question of 'were children better behaved prior to 1965, and the introduction of the Comprehensive Education Act, than they are post 1965?' is a matter for conjecture. We don't really want to get embroiled in a debate about the virtues of comprehensive education but it certainly changed the shape of secondary education in the UK by getting rid of the tripartite system of grammar, technical and secondary modern schools and providing educational opportunities for all children; not dividing them up at an early age into different 'opportunity groups' on the basis of a questionable instrument of selection. The cynical view of the old grammar school system is that it set out to educate the best and forget about the rest (wow, we guess that we did get a bit embroiled in the debate).

Alongside structural changes in the education system, there were changes in the theories underpinning learning. These can be summarised as:

- **behaviourist** theory, which relates to **reactive** learning with the teacher at the centre of the process and where behaviour is controlled by conditioning and reinforcement
- **cognitivist** theory, which relates to **responsive** learning where mental acts are the primary aim and where behaviour is controlled by fostering the learner's self-interests

- **humanist** theory, which is about **reflective** learning, dependent on experience and self-efficacy, and where behaviour is controlled through democratic decision-making.

With the emphasis switching from teacher-controlled to learner-controlled sessions, teacher-imposed discipline was replaced by learner self-discipline, and extrinsic motivational forces (such as imposing threats and bribes) were replaced by the notion of intrinsic motivation (such as encouraging an inner desire to want to learn).

There is little doubt that threats and bribes can induce a short-term change in behaviour, but it may also have the effect of deterring the learner from developing a commitment to positive values. Alfie Kohn, in *Punished by Rewards* (1999), discusses how in a consequence-based classroom children are led to ask 'what does the teacher want me to do, and what happens if I don't do it?'. In a reward-based classroom, they're led to ask 'what does the teacher want me to do, and what do I get for doing it?'. Kohn argues that threats and bribes are simply two sides of the same coin and that children should be encouraged to ask, 'What kind of person do I want to be?' or 'What kind of classroom do we want to have?'.

One of your esteemed authors (we won't say which one) has clear recollections of the date 3 September 1962 and his first day in secondary school.

Example 1.5: A costly DEtour

Anon's class was based in Room D and his first science lesson was in Room E. OK, this may not inspire you to want to take in any of the advice we offer in this book, but he got lost! As everyone piled out to make the 2-metre trek (6'7" in those days) from Room D to the next room in the corridor, he had to make a detour to the toilets at the other end of the corridor. When he came out, he tells us that it was like the *Mary Celeste*: no one in sight.

He was never late for classes again but the humiliation that was heaped upon him as he tried to explain what had happened to a not-too-impressed teacher and his classmates laughing at him, stayed with him for a long time.

Would teachers react differently to his predicament now? We're not sure. We suspect that there is something comical about someone not realising that Room D was next door to Room E but, then again, if it was never explained to him that the rooms were in alphabetical order, is it totally fair to assume that someone, even someone as bright as he was (or so he claims), should know this is the case? We don't expect the teacher to have congratulated him for making it eventually to his class but we do question his behaviour in belittling him.

Demanding obedience through reward and punishment strategies doesn't really encourage learners to work their way through a problem or for teachers to question why there is a problem in the first place and what they could have done to prevent it happening.

Going back to the myth, was it easier to control behaviour in the pre-comprehensive school era? The answer is probably 'yes'. Was the process of achieving obedience through threats and bribes the most effective way of helping children to develop into good learners and good citizens? The answer is probably 'no'.

SUMMARY OF PART 1

In Part 1, we have tried to establish the context for challenging behaviour by examining what we mean by the term, some of the theories that underpin this, and by dispelling some of the myths that have grown up around the subject. The key points to emerge from this are:

- Recognise that challenging behaviour can be intimidatory (violent or abusive), inappropriate (persistently annoying) or passive (non-engaging).
- Accept that it can occur when you least or most expect it and that you can be a contributory factor to it occurring.
- Believe that you can escalate or de-escalate the disruption by inappropriate or appropriate actions.
- Accept that acting aggressively or passively may get you results in the short term, but always trying for a win–win resolution when dealing with challenging behaviour will work better in the long term.
- Know what sources of power you have access to as a teacher. Decide whether you are using them in a positive or negative manner. Identify who in your organisation exercises power and what can you learn from them.
- Don't feel that you should always be deceitful or ruthless as a teacher but do accept that you should be able to play the game in the best interests of your organisation and its learners.
- Don't take your responsibilities as a role model lightly but recognise that you are not infallible.

PART 2

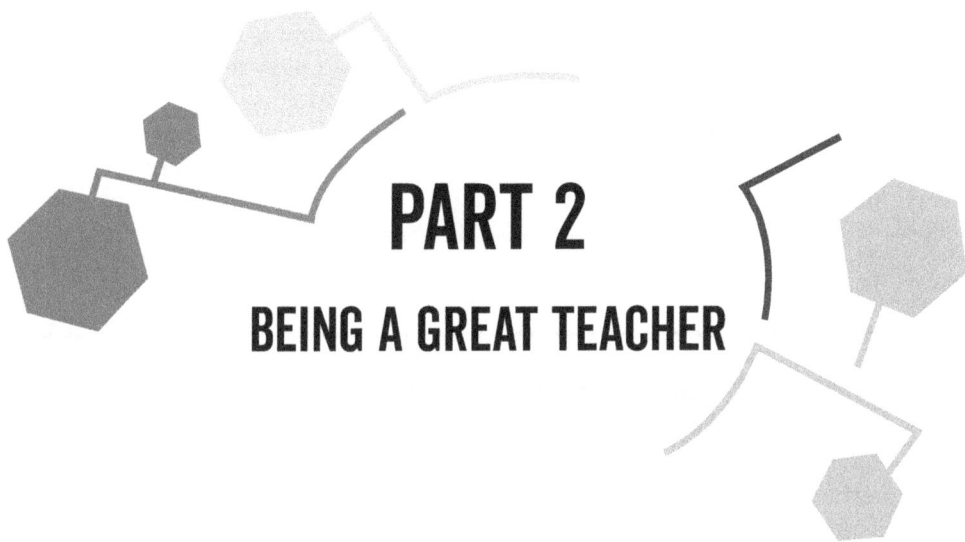

BEING A GREAT TEACHER

Of course, there is no simple blueprint for how to be a great teacher. There are many factors that will impact on your aspirations to be great. These include: *context variables*, such as the environment, resources, class size, timing and subject matter; and *characteristic variables*, such as the gender, age, experience of learners, their motivation to learn and the match between their learning styles and your teaching preferences.

The journey towards greatness is just that; it's a journey, not a destination. Remember that although the map for the journey is not a true indication of the terrain you will be travelling over, there are some important navigational points on the map that you need to understand, especially from the bumps and hollows that you will face when dealing with challenging behaviour. These are:

1. Your rights as a teacher.
2. Your own default position when dealing with challenging behaviour.
3. How to plan your classroom effectively and control space.
4. How to create a first and lasting impression on your learners.
5. What approaches you need to work on to deal with conflict in the class.
6. Who you can turn to for help.
7. How to support learners with special educational needs or disabilities.
8. How to support victims of abuse.
9. How to support learners who are victims of radicalisation.

2.1 KNOW YOUR RIGHTS AS A TEACHER

Let's be clear about this – you have rights just as your learners do. In the same way that your organisation and your learners have an expectation that you will behave in a professional manner, so you should expect that no learner be allowed to prevent you from teaching or keep other learners from learning, and that your organisation will support you when you have to deal with challenging behaviour in the classroom.

Read example 2.1 and the two scenarios that emerge from this.

Example 2.1: Confrontation in the classroom

Darren taught IT to a group of 16-18-year-olds. One of his learners, Jacob, a quiet hardworking member of the class, wore his hoodie during lessons. Darren was constantly asking Jacob to remove the hoodie and, frustrated by his refusal, excluded Jacob from the class. Darren's head of department, Helen, explained that excluding Jacob would result in damage to the organisation performance figures and a possible loss in funding and asked that he be allowed to return to class. Despite Darren's objections, Jacob returned and continued to wear his hoodie.

(A) THE DARREN–JACOB SCENARIO

There are two issues here. First, do you feel that Darren was being reasonable in asking Jacob to remove his hoodie? Second, do you feel that Jacob was being reasonable in refusing to remove his hoodie? It seems that both were out to win the confrontation at the expense of the other. Although Jacob won this particular skirmish, the long-term effect on his relationship with Darren may not be conducive to his achieving his long-term learning outcomes. Interactions of this nature rarely end in a win–win situation. It's usually the case that, in the short term, the one who acts more aggressively will win the interaction or the one that acts more passively will lose.

In *Assertive Discipline* (Canter and Canter, 1992), Lee Canter argued that the rights and needs of teachers and learners are best met when both the teacher and the learner clearly communicate their expectations to each other and consistently follow up with appropriate action that never violates the best interests of the other person. He believed that uncertainty over expectations would often lead to passive or aggressive behaviour on the part of the teacher or learner, which in turn would fail to create an optimum teaching or learning environment.

Here are some tips for applying *assertive discipline* in the classroom:

- Discuss with your learners which rules you all feel comfortable with.
- Have a small number of *given rules*, such as non-threatening behaviour and respect for others' views, that you are not willing to compromise on.
- Be willing to compromise on rules that learners might feel are unreasonable.
- Agree what are acceptable negative consequences (sanctions) for non-compliance with the rules.
- Agree what are acceptable positive consequences (rewards) for compliance with the rules.
- Write up the rules and give everyone (including your line management) a copy and/or display these in a prominent position.
- If anyone infringes the rules, make them aware that it is *their* rules they are breaking.
- Don't forget to catch someone out doing something good. A simple nod of appreciation when Jacob doesn't wear the hoodie will go a long way.

(B) THE DARREN–HELEN SCENARIO

The Darren–Jacob scenario is a common situation of lower-level disruption that could have involved the learner chewing gum or texting a message to someone. Before responding to the situation, you need to know what your organisation's policies are on discipline. Although Helen's approach could be argued to be more to do with outcomes and finances than it was with behaviour policy, if there is zero tolerance for any form of disruption then you need to consider whether you are working in the education or criminal justice system. If, on the other hand, anything goes, it's highly unlikely that anything meaningful will be achieved in the class, and things may even degenerate into chaos. We guess that somewhere in the middle of the two scenarios is where you want to be situated.

Your own values will be important here but be careful about imposing or refusing to impose something that is contrary to school, local educational or national policy. The wearing of the niqab in schools in France was recently banned. Arguments in favour of this ban included threats to national security and exam fraud. Arguments against the ban included disrespect of cultural values and infringement of civil liberties. We suspect that it's a debate that will rage on, causing no end of friction amongst communities. There is no easy solution. If national government, local education authority or individual school policy dictates that something is not allowed, then if you disagree strongly with the policy, you either have to comply with it, challenge it through appropriate means or resign your post there.

Before taking whatever action you feel the situation dictates, complete the *Bostin Performance Questionnaire* (BPQ) in Appendix 1. This will help you to think about the issues that you feel are important and compare this with your organisation's performance rating on that issue. If a score on the left-hand side of the questionnaire (Importance) is greater than the corresponding one on the right-hand side of the questionnaire (Performance), there is a clear area for improvement in how the organisation is performing on that issue. If the score on the left-hand side of the questionnaire is less than the corresponding one on the right-hand side of the questionnaire, there are signs that the organisation may be devoting too many resources to dealing with that issue.

Getting other stakeholders in your organisation to complete the BPQ will give the organisation an excellent appraisal of how well they are performing in terms of behaviour management from different viewpoints in the organisation. If you are puzzled as to where the term *bostin* comes from, it's taken from a term, *tay arf bostin*, from two of the authors' home neck of the woods, meaning something that is excellent. It's also a variation of the *Boston Performance Matrix*, which is widely used in organisational research.

2.2 KNOW YOUR OWN DEFAULT POSITION WHEN DEALING WITH CHALLENGING BEHAVIOUR

Are you a firm disciplinarian (a *behaviourist*) or the classroom democrat (a *humanist*)? Do you believe that the punishment should fit the crime (a *reactivist*) or that prevention is better than cure (a *proactivist*)? Knowing what your default position is in this respect is important because it will (a) encourage you to be consistent in how you deal with situations and (b) provide the basis for reflection on the appropriateness of your approach to classroom interactions.

Before reading the rest of this section, complete the questionnaires in Appendices 2 and 3.

What follows are two entries that will make sense of the results in your questionnaires.

1. DEALING WITH THE RESULTS OF APPENDIX 2

Douglas McGregor's X–Y theory (1985) was originally used to categorise managers. It can however be applied equally well to teachers. McGregor's ideas are based on a set of assumptions that represent extreme views of behaviour and reactions to these. The views can be summarised as follows:

- **Theory X teachers** believe that learners dislike work and will avoid it if possible, and that they lack interest in the subject and are unambitious. They believe that learners prefer to be told what to do. X teachers rely on coercion and external stimuli to promote a change in behaviour. They believe that it is their responsibility to structure learning programmes and energise their learners.
- **Theory Y teachers** believe that learners find work stimulating and interesting, are fascinated by learning new subjects and are keen to use newly acquired skills and knowledge. Y teachers rely on learners working well on their own initiative. They believe that it is their responsibility to create a climate where self-motivated learners will flourish.

On this interpretation, it is important to stress that not all *X-rated* teachers are bad and not all *Y-rated* teachers are good. There's room for both approaches, given the characteristics of the learners and the context in which learning is taking place. Other issues, such as the subject matter and the time frame for learning, need to be taken into account.

In the mid-18th century, Jean-Jacques Rousseau presented his theories on education in the story of *Emile* (1911), about Rousseau's tutor–student relationship with Emile. *Emile* was a landmark contribution to education theory but needs to be understood in the context in which it was written. This was during a time when society was built on people who enjoyed dominating others for personal gain and people who either passively accepted this domination and a life of servitude or resented those that wielded power over them and revolted. As Emile's tutor, Rousseau was faced with the dichotomy of not wanting to have an overt position of power over Emile but covertly exerting influence over his education.

Rousseau's theory of education was based on a belief in the inherent goodness of human beings and the effect of society in corrupting them. He argued that bringing up children in harmony with nature and its laws would facilitate learning and preserve their goodness.

His thinking is based on three key principles:

* People should be able to learn what they want to learn.
* They should be able to do this when they want to.
* Teaching should be based on discovery, enriched with the covert guidance of the teacher.

Rousseau's focus on nature, on the need to develop opportunities for new experiences and reflection and on the dynamic provided by each individual's development remains the cornerstone of modern pedagogical thinking. We're not going to set out a series of steps here as we think you need to reflect on whether you feel the treatment of Emile was characteristic of an X teacher or a Y teacher. Your answer to this will help you decide how to use the theory. We are going to suggest that you watch Lewis Gilbert's (2005) film based on Willy Russell's play, *Educating Rita*, to give you some food for thought on this.

EDUCATING RITA

In *Educating Rita*, Rita, played by Julie Walters, wants to better herself by studying literature. Her tutor, Frank, played by Michael Caine, describes his teaching ability as 'appalling, but good enough for appalling students'. Issues of power and influence are common themes throughout the film as both Rita and Frank struggle to cope with personal and professional difficulties. The essence of the film is about Frank's attempts to teach Rita to value her own insights whilst still being able to pass the exams. Does he succeed? Watch the film to find out.

Here are some questions that you might now want to ask yourself:

- Does Rita succeed or fail? You may need to reconcile your thoughts on what constitutes success and failure. Stepping out on to the Centre Court at Wimbledon (in my dreams) is a saying from Kipling that equates success and failure as both being 'imposters'. What do you think he means by this?
- Does the end result justify the actions that Frank takes? You will certainly have to spend some time thinking this one through. Machiavelli claims that the 'ends always justify the means'. Do you agree?
- Have you ever played out the role of Rita as a learner? If so, how do you feel about it now?
- Have you ever played out the role of Frank as a teacher? If so, how do you feel about it now?

It's possible that, as a result of answering some of the above questions, you may consider aspects of Rousseau's teaching to be unethical, but there are some compelling ideas in Rousseau's work around the freedom to learn that are worth considering.

Don't assume that your default position as a teacher should always be to embrace Theory Y to the total exclusion of Theory X. The reality is that you may have to deal with learners who need to be directed and, on occasions, coerced. If this does happen, your style will be about command and control. Try not to let this slip into being intimidating or threatening. You may get a quick result from this but you can forget any long-term development. The other side of the coin is the danger you run of being seen as weak and a bit of a pushover, if you are too compliant with the needs of your learners. It may be that the ideal is an approach somewhere between the two extremes, where cooperation and compromise dovetail with command and control.

2. DEALING WITH THE RESULTS OF APPENDIX 3

Understanding what your default position (proactive or reactive) is in dealing with challenging behaviour when it occurs is important. The best place to start when seeking to develop a positive learning environment, however, is to try to prevent disruptive behaviour happening in the first place. Let's look at the Montessorian approach to proactive behaviour management.

Dr Maria Montessori (Hainstock, 1997) founded a theory of education that has had a profound influence on the lives of thousands of children throughout the world since the beginning of the 20th century. Montessori believed in the importance of educating the senses before educating the intellect. Her theories were developed as a result of her time as a physician working with children in Italian slums who were categorised as *uneducable*. She rejected the reactivist's approach to behaviour management through rewards and punishment and focused on developing exercises that prepared children to behave appropriately by developing their awareness of the environment and the greater good.

Example 2.2 considers a fairly common situation involving two 7-year-olds in the playground.

Example 2.2: Sorry seems to be the hardest word

Max takes Ed's favourite toy off him. Ed hits Max. Max starts to cry. When their teacher asks what happened, Ed says that 'Max took my toy off me'. The teacher asks Ed to say 'sorry for upsetting Max'. Ed looks defiantly at the teacher and shakes his head. 'I'm waiting', the teacher says, 'Do you want me to go to the head?' 'Sorry', Ed says. 'Now say it as if you mean it', the teacher says. A more contrite Ed says 'Sorry, Max'. 'That's better', the teacher says, 'now carry on playing nicely'.

This is not an uncommon situation and not an uncommon way of dealing with it. We suspect that most teachers and parents would have dealt with it in exactly the same way. Making Ed say 'sorry', however, is like giving him a *get out of jail free card*. The teacher congratulating him for saying 'sorry' almost legitimises his actions. What exactly has he learned? He has learned that saying 'sorry' gets him out of trouble and into his teacher's good books. Of course, in Max's eyes, Ed getting scolded by the teacher legitimises his actions in taking Ed's toy off him.

Let's assume that later on, in the same playground session, Ed hits another learner.

'What did I tell you about upsetting other children?' his teacher says. 'Sorry', says Ed. 'Sorry is not good enough', his teacher says. 'One more time and you will go to the head.'

Again, there is no criticism of the way that the teacher has dealt with the situation. She has imposed a *three strikes and you're out* rule.

Let's assume it's a week later. It's the same playground, the same children and Ed and Max are pushing and shoving each other.

'Right you two, I've told you before, now go to the head', their teacher says. 'But you haven't given us our two warnings', Ed says.

From the experiences of the previous week, Ed makes a fair assumption that he can't be punished until he's abused the rule three times. He clearly knows the rules but he doesn't learn compassion or responsibility for his actions from his teacher's handling of the situation.

Montessorian educators believe that young children behave in hurtful ways towards others because they have not yet developed the means to manage intense feelings that sometimes overwhelm them. They recognise that young children require help in understanding the range of feelings they experience and in recognising their feelings by naming them and trying to express them, thus making a connection verbally between the event and the feeling. In the Ed–Max situation, the teacher might say to Ed, 'Max took your toy, didn't he, and you were enjoying playing with it. You didn't like it when he took it, did you? Did it make you feel angry? Is that why you hit him?' By following this approach, as children get older, the expectation is that they will be more able to verbalise their feelings, talking through for themselves the feelings that motivated the behaviour.

An important principle here is the understanding that self-management of intense emotions, especially of anger, only happens when the brain has developed neurological systems to manage the physiological processes that take place when triggers activate responses of anger or fear. Montessori argues that the best way to help this process is by offering support, calming the child who is angry as well as the one who has been hurt by the behaviour. By helping the child to return to a normal state rather than engaging in punitive responses to their rage and risking aggravating the situation, Montessori claims that we are helping the brain to develop the physiological response system that will help the child be able to manage their own feelings and therefore their behaviour.

In Montessorian schools, children as young as 6 are made aware of 'truth and justice' and the need to think before they act and to look at the big picture. This is done through the process of 'Active Listening', where the teacher helps the children to take turns in listening and in explaining their conflict and feelings. After all sides have explained their take on a conflict, they are then encouraged to consider how the other side(s) perceives the conflict. The children are then guided though solving the problem together. Besides learning to work together, children learn to look at the 'big picture' before making judgements. Through this process, they discover that most conflicts occur not as a result of the actual meanness of others, but due to misunderstanding and peer pressure.

Example 2.3 is a classic example of encouraging empathy in action.

Example 2.3: A lesson well learned

Jane Elliot taught a class of all white 9-year-olds. The day after Martin Luther King was shot, she wanted to show her class how it felt being discriminated against and bullied because of a physical characteristic. She divided her class into blue-eyed and non-blue-eyed children. She told them that the blue-eyed children were brighter and better than the others. The blue-eyed children started acting in an arrogant manner and deriding the others who became confused and withdrawn.

Jane reversed the process the following day and found that the non-blue-eyed children then became the arrogant ones. By using role play to get the children to experience prejudice first-hand and to discuss what effect it had on them, she was hoping to get the children to understand the importance of tolerance of one another.

Years later, many of her former pupils confessed that the exercise had had a profound effect on their thoughts about segregation and bullying.

Young children are often told 'it's wrong to bully other children'. In the Montessorian approach, they are asked 'why is it wrong to bully other children?' In this way they are helped to think about the ramifications of their behaviour. If they do bully someone and a reaction is necessary, the natural and logical consequences are followed whenever possible – for example, not being able to play or work with children whom they have been hurtful or mean to.

Although it is wrong to assume that there is no discipline within Montessorian schools, it's a self-discipline that is fostered through a belief in the greater good and not one based on fear of punishments or desire for rewards. In the Montessorian approach, all staff, volunteers and students are required to use positive strategies for handling any inconsiderate behaviour by helping children find solutions in ways which are appropriate for the children's ages and stages of development. Such solutions might include, for example, acknowledgement of feelings, explanation as to what was not acceptable and supporting children to gain control of their feelings so that they can learn a more appropriate response.

Being a Montessorian teacher, however, may only be partially under your control. Here are some suggestions:

- Make sure that there are enough popular toys and resources and sufficient activities available so that children are meaningfully occupied without the need for unnecessary conflict over sharing and waiting for turns.
- Only when there is a risk to physical injury to children or adults and/or serious damage to property should physical restraint, such as holding, be used.
- Never use physical punishment, such as smacking or shaking. Never send children out of the room by themselves or use a 'naughty' chair. Never threaten children with these.
- Teach them to understand the outcomes of any inconsiderate action on their part and support them in learning how to cope more appropriately.
- Exercise restraint and avoid shouting or raising your voice in a threatening way to respond to children's inconsiderate behaviour. If tantrums, biting or fighting are frequent, try to find out the underlying cause – such as a change or upheaval at home, or frequent change of carers. Sometimes a child has not settled in well and the behaviour may be the result of 'separation anxiety'.
- Support each child in developing self-esteem, confidence and feelings of competence.

- **S**upport each child in developing a sense of belonging in the group, so that they feel valued and welcome.
- **O**nly impose sanctions when the behaviour is likely to cause serious harm or distress to the victim.
- **R**ecognise and appreciate when the child displays considerate behaviour such as kindness and willingness to share, and avoid creating situations in which children receive adult attention only in return for inconsiderate behaviour.
- **I**n cases of serious misbehaviour, such as racial or other abuse, make clear immediately the unacceptability of the behaviour and attitudes, by means of explanations rather than personal blame.

If your head is spinning over whether you are a *proactive behaviourist* or a *reactive humanist*, then the model in Figure 2.1 will help you make sense of this. The model is represented by a window frame divided into four quadrants. Each quadrant, resembling a window pane, depicts how you approach behaviour management depending on where you stand on the Behaviourist–Humanist (X–Y) scale and on the Proactive–Reactive (P–R) scale.

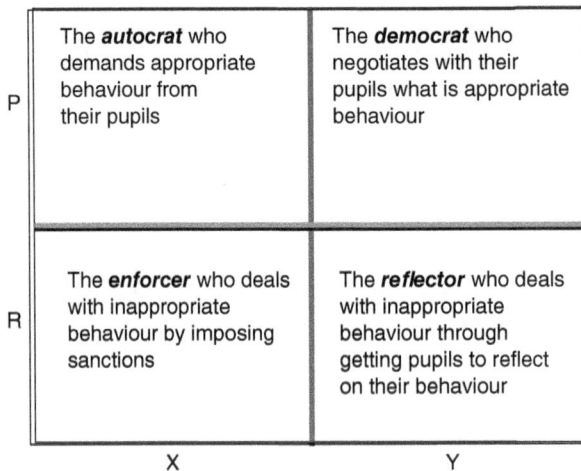

	X	Y
P	The **autocrat** who demands appropriate behaviour from their pupils	The **democrat** who negotiates with their pupils what is appropriate behaviour
R	The **enforcer** who deals with inappropriate behaviour by imposing sanctions	The **reflector** who deals with inappropriate behaviour through getting pupils to reflect on their behaviour

Figure 2.1   The BOVAL windows *Source:* © Bob Bates

The BOVAL windows will help you determine what your default position is. Plot your scores from Appendix 2 (X–Y) on the horizontal axis and from Appendix 3 (P–R) on the vertical axis. For example, someone with an X score of 60 and an R score of 20 will have a frame that looks something like the following frame, indicating that their tendency is towards that of the *autocrat*.

P (80)

R (20)

X (60)   Y (40)

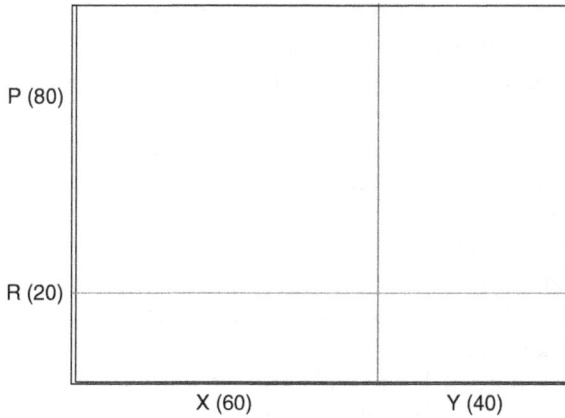

Other frames could resemble any one of those in the following:

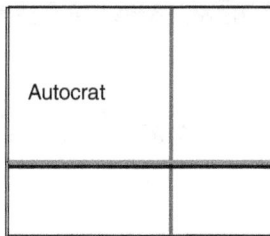

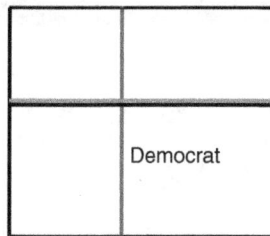

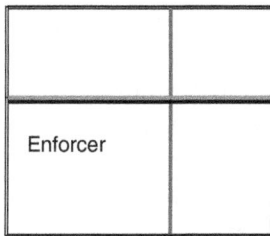

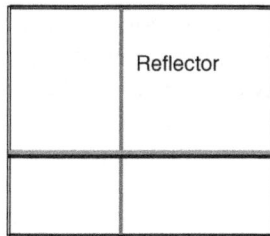

Autocrat

Democrat

Enforcer

Reflector

The more honest and accurate you are by working out the scores and plotting them on a graphical representation of the window, the more accurate the assessment of your default position (the largest window in the frame) will be. Which size frame is best depends on the context in which teaching is taking place. For example:

- The **autocrat** thrives in a situation where there is a class of immature learners or where there are health and safety issues and potential hazards in the classroom that should be avoided. They are less comfortable in situations where learners are given complete freedom to learn.
- The **democrat** is more at home with more mature learners who have demonstrated a capacity for self-discipline. They are less comfortable working in organisations where rules are strictly enforced.
- The **enforcer** is best suited to situations where learners react better to clear guidelines about what is right and what is wrong, and the consequences attached to infringing or complying with the guidelines. They are less comfortable when classroom rules are negotiable.
- The **reflector** is more at home with learners who are capable of reflecting on their behaviour and capable of determining what the consequences of their behaviour should be. They are less comfortable where guidelines about what is right and what is wrong are imposed by the organisation.

> **Hot Tip**: Knowing what your default position is will allow you to make changes that are more appropriate to the context in which you are teaching.

2.3 KNOW HOW TO PLAN YOUR CLASSROOM EFFECTIVELY AND CONTROL SPACE

What does a well-planned classroom look like? The simple answer is that there isn't a single template for this. Classrooms that promote good behaviour and facilitate effective learning exist in many forms and are judged, not by fashionable notions as to how they should be set up, but by what they achieve.

The learning environment is manipulated by a thoughtful teacher to promote effective learning and good behaviour. It's therefore worth spending time planning your classroom and periodically reviewing its effectiveness. Rather than attempt to provide ready answers, we aim to prompt you to consider issues which are designed to help you shape your own effective learning environment.

Your classroom plan, however well considered, will not in itself bring about good learning behaviour and achievement. The classroom is an expression of the teacher and as such it needs to reflect their personality, strengths and philosophy. Only then will the teacher be able to function effectively.

To be able to function effectively within your classroom, you must feel comfortable within it. When planning a classroom, it is important to consider your preferred teaching style.

Just as the classroom needs to reflect your teaching style, it must also accommodate the needs of the learners. The environment must enable your teaching to capture their attention and engage them in learning, including those with the most challenging

Example 2.4: Actions can have unforeseen outcomes

Early in Satvir's career, she was perhaps too open to 'new' ideas, which on one particular occasion brought about a radical overhaul of the seating plan within her classroom. However, rather than facilitate improvements, standards declined because the 'improved' layout was incompatible with her preferred method of delivery.

Example 2.5: Design a solution to fit the problem

Faced with a 'lively' class, a colleague of Adam suggested putting desks in rows to limit unfocused, disruptive behaviour. The new layout lasted a week. Apart from the fact that some members of the class still found many ways of disrupting learning, the arrangement was just not suited to his preference for interacting with small groups and promoting group discussion. It also curtailed his freedom of movement around the classroom and therefore his ability to deal quickly and non-confrontationally with poor behaviour and provide support for individual learners when required.

behaviour. It is on this basis that the effectiveness of your classroom must be judged by you and not by others. Adam's colleague in example 2.5 was well intentioned in her recommendations but her suggestion didn't work. Therefore, step back from time to time to assess how successful your classroom is in enabling you to teach effectively.

Each new class offers a fresh set of challenges, depending on the characteristics of the learners; modifications may therefore need to be made to the classroom environment. Gather as much information as you can on the learners. For example, are there any learners who pose particular demands or who have special needs?

Example 2.6: Doing what is best, not what is desired

Val had two year 8 learners (they were twin sisters) who had been assessed as having Attention Deficit Hyperactivity Disorder (ADHD). They promised Val that they would

(Continued)

(Continued)

behave if she allowed them to sit together. After several minutes of pleading from the two twins, Val relented and, on the basis that they behaved, she allowed them to sit together. The decision was a disaster and, after a series of several disruptions, the twins were separated. At first, they both resented this but they eventually settled down and, without the distraction of their sister, each became more focused in their learning behaviour.

When planning a classroom, there are certain conditions that need to be met in order to fulfil the requirements of learners.

CATERING FOR LEARNERS' PHYSICAL WELL-BEING

An obvious requirement, but one that is not always easy to achieve for all learners within the classroom is well-being: poor ventilation, too much or too little heat or light, and unsuitable furniture can all affect how well we feel and our ability to learn. Within a classroom, there can be a variety of contrasting conditions. Some learners can be sweltering working near to a heat source, whilst in another part of the classroom others are dithering in draughty areas. Do whatever you can to provide optimum learning conditions for all learners.

There is a vast range of challenges to do with learners with sensory and physical functioning. At one end of the spectrum there are learners with chronic illnesses that are not life-threatening and have symptoms that can be addressed with medication or rest. At the other end, there are learners who have progressive, life-threatening conditions, with little or no control over their physical functioning. Support in this respect covers both the medical and the educational. A learner with diabetes, for example, may function perfectly well if they are reminded to take their medication or allowed snack or rest periods during a lesson to keep their blood sugar up. Someone with severe sight or hearing loss, however, may have no other medical issues but may need specialist equipment to help keep pace with their peers. Because of the difference in the degree of severity of a specific condition or the long-term/short-term nature of the condition, the symptoms, challenges and strategies for dealing with different conditions may vary significantly.

CATERING FOR LEARNERS' SOCIAL AND EMOTIONAL WELL-BEING

All learners have a right to be free from emotional stress and for their learning to be unimpeded by the actions of others. There needs to be positive encouragement and support, providing opportunities to learn with and from their peers. In the same way, learners whose behaviour is liable to cause stress or anxiety to others need to be protected from their own worst instincts, if they are to make any progress whilst they are being taught by you. Where they sit within the room therefore demands careful consideration of their neurological or psychological state of mind.

Neurology and psychology are closely related in that they are disciplines that focus on the functions and disorders of the brain. The disorders arising from each can be distinguished by the following definitions:

- A **neurological** disorder is when something happens to hinder or prevent the development of areas of the brain that control movement or sensory perception. This includes conditions such as Down syndrome, autism and dyslexia.
- A **psychological** disorder is a disorder of the mind involving thoughts, behaviours and emotions that cause either the self or others significant distress. This includes conditions such as schizophrenia, attachment disorder and depression.

Both sets of disorders can be wide-ranging, affecting someone's physical, cognitive, emotional or behavioural states. They have various causes, complications and outcomes. Some disorders can be treated, whilst others are permanent. Some disorders are present at birth (congenital), others emerge during infancy and adolescence, whereas some remain dormant until adulthood. Some disorders may be very limited in their functional effects, whilst others may involve substantial disability and subsequent support needs.

Identifying brain-related disorders in learners can be difficult with many conditions, such as ADHD and autism, not being diagnosed until later childhood. In some cases, identifying the cause of a disorder can be complicated because they have a variety of symptoms that make it difficult to associate with any one condition.

PROVIDING LEARNERS WITH ENOUGH SPACE

We all need and value personal space. Few of us respond well when our personal space is severely restricted. Learners also need sufficient space in which to work, thus avoiding unnecessary contact with others and thereby curtailing opportunities for possible conflict, particularly when the conditions for this already exist in the form of learners with challenging behaviour.

Rarely is there enough space to set up the ideal classroom. Usually it is a matter of finding the most effective compromise. In considering how to maximise space for learning, start with how much space you and your own possessions and equipment occupy. Ask yourself whether it is all necessary and if the space could be better employed in ensuring learners have sufficient space to work unimpeded by others and to move around the room with the minimum disruption to others, including lining up and entering and exiting the room. It is also imperative for the teacher to be able to move freely around the room in order to support learners as unobtrusively as possible.

This also applies when delivering sanctions or issuing praise as the impact is likely to be greater if you are able to do this less publicly, thereby avoiding the possibility of a defensive or aggressive reaction. If possible, consider creating a more private space within the classroom where breaches of the behaviour code can be addressed with individuals so that there can be physical space between teacher and learner, preferably on the same level (at eye level) so as not to appear 'threatening'. When planning your classroom, be creative and try to provide solutions which make optimum use of the space available to facilitate good learning behaviour.

Decide whether you are going to create an area where the attention of all the class can be focused when required. Your presence in a specified location will then create an expectation for everyone to give you their attention; this can be a real timesaver. If designating such an area, consider whether it should be close to your base, if you have one, or near to a whiteboard, and ensure that it is away from sources of distraction such as windows. Also think about your own comfort, as you could be spending some time there.

For teachers of younger learners, consideration might also be given to creating a space where they can all gather to listen to the teacher, receive feedback on or share their learning with one another. If you feel this is a beneficial feature for your classroom, it will need to be factored into your overall plan.

The organisation and layout of the classroom may need to change depending on the subject being taught, for example a lesson in personal, social and health education may require floor space, or tables may be put together in different configurations for group work. Some learners may require more space than others, due to physical, emotional, behavioural or educational needs. You may need to accommodate other adults employed to teach within your room: these could be operating under your jurisdiction or may be peripatetic and will often be working with small groups.

CREATING A POSITIVE CLIMATE FOR LEARNING

You need to take into account the characteristics of the learners within the class. The age of the learners will go a long way to determining how your classroom is organised. What is appropriate for a young adult is unlikely to suit children at the start of their school lives. Maturity usually develops with age, but they do not necessarily go hand in hand.

Example 2.7: There is rarely a one-size-fits-all solution

One year, Zoe taught a Year 4 class of sociable, enthusiastic learners whose self-motivation led her to modify the classroom over the year to include freedom of movement, access to materials and private study areas. The following year she was given responsibility for a Year 6 class. Buoyed with the success of the previous year, she assumed a similar environment would be appropriate for an older year group. It only took a short time to discover this was not the case; as a group they were almost polar opposites of the previous class, lacking social cohesion and being influenced by a group of pupils with challenging behaviour. They lacked the maturity and self-motivation to profit from learning opportunities being presented in the way they were; rather, they used them as opportunities to misbehave. Zoe quickly changed the classroom to better cater for their immaturity and lack of independence.

SEATING PLANS

The arrangement of seating is constrained by the space available. The best arrangements will make use of the space available rather than crowd it. That said, seating arrangements are numerous and vary from strictly regimented rows of desks, with each learner having an appointed place, to very informal arrangements of work surfaces where learners do not have a permanent designated place, this being determined by the particular activity being undertaken at the time, or by the learner's own choice. No one arrangement provides a guaranteed solution to managing behaviour. The aforementioned experiment of sitting learners in rows did not bring about the desired result, in part because the seating arrangement actually restricted quick and easy movement to the source of misbehaviour, meaning that any reproach was broadcast from a distance for everyone to hear. Because there was an 'audience', this subsequently led to confrontations with some learners. It also made the delivery of praise less personal and consequently either reduced its impact or rendered it ineffective.

Whether you wish to designate learners to particular seats will depend on your method of teaching plus the age and maturity of learners, which may mean that you do not always adhere to the same policy. It is worth remembering that however much you wish to encourage independence, learners do not always make the best choices about who they work with and there are certain combinations of individuals who are best kept apart. If, because of behaviour, you feel it wise to designate individual learners to particular places or to isolate them from other learners, then try to do this with sensitivity for the individuals concerned to avoid negative attitudes and possible negative behaviour.

The seating plan that you select will need to reflect your preferred teaching style. If you prefer teaching small groups and welcome learner interaction then clusters of tables would appear to be more suitable; however, if you have a more didactic style then arranging learners in rows, or in a horseshoe layout, would appear more appropriate.

Whatever arrangement you have for seating learners, it is important to retain sight-lines in order to ensure eye contact with learners as required. This is particularly important when talking to the whole class. Therefore, if some learners are seated with their backs to you when you are talking, they need room to turn their chairs to face you without causing disruption to others.

The use of information technology can influence seating plans. For instance, when using electronic whiteboards it would seem logical to orient desks in rows, with all learners facing the whiteboard.

FURNITURE

There may be little choice over what furniture you use in your classroom, but nevertheless it could be a useful exercise to undertake an audit of what you have. How much of what you have do you actually need? Remember that your prime aim is to create as much space as you can for effective learning. A glance at a catalogue shows that there is a range of desks, tables, chairs and storage units available. If you are fortunate enough to be able to furnish your classroom then select furniture best suited to your teaching style and priorities for learning. Primarily, work surfaces and chairs need to be an appropriate size for learners to allow them to work comfortably.

It is rare for a classroom to have the storage capacity and equipment that you would like. Your classroom organisation will therefore usually be a compromise between what you would like to do and what is possible. Many factors will be beyond your control and you will just have to make the best of the situation, but if you can effect any changes that will enhance your capacity to organise learning and behaviour effectively then do not hesitate to do so. You could well find that a well-justified appeal to a senior figure will not fall on deaf ears.

Depending on the age of learners or the subject being taught, some classrooms require a large amount of equipment, much of which needs to be stored. When storing equipment, consider its impact on the space for learning. We have visited enough classrooms to know that some teachers struggle with this issue, resulting in classrooms that appear disorderly and therefore send out the wrong messages to learners. A key question to ask yourself is: what do the learners and I really need? This is not as simple as it may appear, for consideration needs to be given to a number of factors including environmental issues.

When you have decided on essential equipment, consider the most effective storage to maximise space but also to give access to learners, minimising the potential for disruption, particularly by those who are looking for such opportunities. It is for you to decide on the degree of access that you wish learners to have to equipment. This could depend on their maturity and on them being provided with clear rules and procedures, which in turn will dictate the kind of storage units and/or areas that you have, and where they are located. The types of units that you inherit in your room need not dictate how they are used; doors can be removed and open units and shelves curtained off.

DÉCOR

Your classroom should be giving positive messages about learning. A cluttered, drab, uninformative environment is no stimulant to learning or good behaviour. It suggests that if you, the teacher, can't be bothered, why should the learners? It is unlikely that your room will be refurnished very often, but you can always ask, and should your room be allocated for redecoration, give some thought to colour schemes that create the required ambience for a calm but stimulating environment.

Put wall space to good use. Display information that reminds learners of expectations for behaviour and learning by exhibiting rules and procedures that have been agreed. Use display to arouse interest, to provide information relating to current teaching and learning and to celebrate learners' achievements by exhibiting their work. Such displays will need to be updated regularly to ensure their relevance. Whatever forms of display you employ, provide learners with clear examples of expected standards regarding content and presentation.

Take time out to visualise your perfect classroom. It may be an impossible dream. In reality, space will probably be restricted and the furniture you have at your disposal will be less than ideal. However, once you have accepted the constraints of your classroom, you can give some consideration to how you are going to make best use of what's available.

Let's just reflect on your classroom planning. Put yourself in the position of a learner at the school. Here are some questions that will shape what they think about the room they are working in:

- Is there poor ventilation or too much or too little heat or light?
- Is the furniture comfortable?
- Do I feel free from emotional stress?
- Is my learning going to be impeded, for example by the actions of others?
- Can I see/hear the teacher without having to stretch?
- Can I move around the room with minimum disruption to others?
- Do I have sufficient space in which to work?
- Does the décor in the room give positive messages about learning, or is it cluttered and drab?

If you are happy with your answers to those questions then you will be satisfied that you have a good classroom set-up. If not then do something about it.

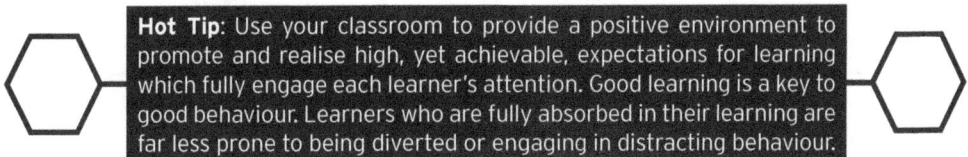

> **Hot Tip**: Use your classroom to provide a positive environment to promote and realise high, yet achievable, expectations for learning which fully engage each learner's attention. Good learning is a key to good behaviour. Learners who are fully absorbed in their learning are far less prone to being diverted or engaging in distracting behaviour.

2.4 KNOW HOW TO CREATE A FIRST AND LASTING IMPRESSION ON YOUR LEARNERS

We can all remember the first time we visited a particular hotel, restaurant, friend's house, solicitor's office, supermarket or school. The reasons we were there are multifarious and the list would be as long as a ball of string. Let's look at two of those examples – supermarket and school. We arrive at our chosen venue. Let's just ponder on what we first saw, thought, felt or did. In other words, what was it that was so striking that we can recall it now? Was it the building's immediate attraction – well maintained or shabby? How good was access – easy parking or no on-site provision? Was it signage that we could read and understand – clear or confusing? Was it the people we met – courteous or distant? In this section, we want to look at the importance of creating a good first impression from both a school and a classroom teacher perspective. Both can have a significant impact on the way that learners behave in class.

Let's start with the environment. If we pause just for a moment, we may take stock of the purpose of the building we are visiting and the many issues that could determine what we saw, thought, felt or how we behaved. In our two examples, the supermarket is drawing us in to separate us from our money, so it will be advertising its wares; extolling the virtues of shopping here and not elsewhere; seducing us with offers of discounted prices on a range of goods and services; providing trolleys that we can wheel, sit children in and do handbrake turns with by the baked beans display; and presenting other eye-catching promotions. We are well aware of most of what it is endeavouring to do even before we have navigated the revolving door. It is true that marketing attracts us and makes us feel relaxed and ready to part with our money.

We now switch our attention from the supermarket to the school. For perfectly understandable reasons, it is often impossible to access a school campus without speaking into an entry mouthpiece or swiping a card or pressing a buzzer – this is not being unfriendly or distant but mindful of the dangers of having free access. Safeguarding is more important than tins of baked beans. However, it is important that our first impression is balanced quickly at the door and reception area. This is where the school now has advantages over the supermarket since there are people whom you will meet and converse with immediately. If staff are friendly, courteous, engaging, helpful and convey a feeling of welcome (even if you are an angry parent, a distressed child, a delivery person or an Ofsted inspector), then this will become the first impression and it will last and it will be recalled.

Example 2.8: Memories

Two of us went to the same school (a secondary modern school in the Midlands) and clearly remember our first day there. There was a coal bunker (yes – the boiler was coal-fired in those days) where we were warned that if they didn't like you the fifth-formers would throw you into it (the bunker not the boiler). We wore caps with blips in (little button-type things on the top of the cap). Being de-blipped was a rite of passage and you felt that you didn't belong until some bigger kid had removed your blip. It was almost like you couldn't wait four years until you could threaten some terrified first year by nodding towards the bunker unless they surrendered their blip. By the time that happened, however, the school had converted to oil-fired heating. You may not have been a pupil in the 1960s but can you recall your first day at school?

What else helps? You are in the school on your first day and feel welcome (menacing fifth-formers are kept under control). You see well-displayed work from other children; colourful notices; signs in various languages; people smiling and moving around purposefully. You feel that there is a healthy atmosphere and your initial fears are replaced with an aura of care. Unfortunately, first impressions are not always good ones, so a stern face, tight lips and a barked 'get in line' or 'why aren't you in your classroom?' will also be remembered lastingly. We acknowledge that many schools were built at a time when the niceties of reception space and, sadly, reception attitudes were not good.

Example 2.9: Everyone welcome, or not?

We recently visited a school in London where a notice at the top of the school drive read, 'Parents are not allowed past this point'. Inside the school, the first notice we read was, 'We are a caring community'. Spot the irony.

So, let's rewind. We are inside the supermarket and filling our trolley and ticking off items on our shopping list. Everything is functional. Staff load shelves, point us to the cauliflowers, scan our goods and, as we fold the till receipt, wish us a 'nice day'. They are well trained and, by and large, what you see is what you get. You will be back next week, though advertisements on television indicate a rival might be reducing some of its prices. This will test your loyalty. It might blur your impressions. There is no real emotional connection here. There is however in school and amongst the people working there.

In fact, in good schools, emotional connections abound – some are obvious and others more subliminal. A teacher will face the day as a challenge; (s)he is unlikely to know what will happen. You want everyone to have a 'nice day' and if you enable all around you to have this, you will feel joyful – even if you yourself have not had one. Metaphorically speaking, you've stacked the shelves, arranged the packets of dishwasher tablets, straightened the labels, mopped up a spillage, smiled at an angry customer, reassured a parent separated from her child, rearranged a display, worked long hours, and so on. Every day starts with a first impression and today yours began with a teacher colleague who said your class was noisy. The sense of hurt and injustice stayed with you and, despite trying to improve your yoga breathing and eating a chocolate bar that you vowed to ignore, your overall and lasting impression of the day was negative. First impressions last. Of course, you will bounce back and tomorrow, hopefully, will be a 'nice day'.

We all make judgements all the time and we need to accept that what one person finds acceptable (the 'working' noise in a classroom is healthy), another will find unacceptable ('working noise' reflects poor discipline). We should never underestimate the power of an impression – impressions are not just flights of fancy but are real and can be worked on in relationships, interactions, creations. They can be made solid but they can be reformed, changed and reborn. They are more than just handprints made in wet clay. We should be mindful right from the start of where we want to go before and after the clay solidifies.

Example 2.10: The enforcer

Josie started the first day of the autumn term with a new class. Excitement was high and nerves twanging. She knew that what she did first was important and that every time something new cropped up, she would be dealing with it for the first time. It won't be the last time but first is first. She told the class what the rules were about entering and leaving the classroom. 'It will be orderly', she said. However, as the students were dismissed, one of them pushed past another and dashed off. She knew that if she did nothing, there is no longer a rule and the impression she would be giving was that someone else's rule trumps hers. She knew that she had to make a stand as soon as possible and lay her cards on the table again.

The rule might be a poor one or open to misinterpretation or seemingly irrelevant, but if it isn't enforced, the impression of not being in control is strengthened. This is what lasts. Tomorrow, you have the opportunity to put matters right. Do it and you will be seen as a person who backs up words with action. Do nothing and there is no consistency – your word is not your bond.

Lack of consistency is what drives football fans crazy – one referee shows a red card to a player for a two-footed tackle whilst another shows a yellow and yet another waves play on and still another shows a yellow card to the 'victim' whom he deems to be guilty of simulation. One must acknowledge that there will never be the same outcome for the same incident, even with the use of the Video Assistant

Referee (VAR). For one reason, two incidents cannot be the same – they cannot be morphed into one. Sometimes we see what we want to see. This has to be accepted and the best we can do is constantly strive for consistency of attitude, behaviour and action. So, next time the students enter the classroom, remind them of the rule, of the previous incident and the consequences. Remember that it is good practice to give a brief reminder of and reason for the rule and the possible outcome of having no rule.

When teachers (just as parents and carers) try to be consistent in their relationships with those in their care and those sharing in the care, students will acknowledge this. They will say Ms X or Mr Y or Mrs Z has a reputation for consistency, and will more easily accept their mistakes. A Year 10 student told us recently that his favourite teacher 'works really hard to always be the same, but he can't be because he's only human!' Reputation is an underpinning element of impression.

Example 2.11: Pupils can see right through you

In a Year 6 English lesson, pupils had to describe a member of staff without naming them. The task was preceded by quite a detailed explanation of what libel and slander were! From the first sentence, a girl was quite obviously referring to one of us as she wrote, 'Mr X comes to school wearing Hush Puppies and a string vest...'. Pupils miss nothing.

You can learn a lot about behaviour management by talking to and observing other teachers, but make sure that the advice they give you is sound and suits your own particular style.

Example 2.12: Making an impression

Jack was attending an induction meeting prior to his first day as a teacher in a high school. He had been given a plethora of information about the school and his mentor, Thomas, ended the session by giving him a final piece of advice about behaviour management. 'Start as you mean to go on. Don't give an inch. Give them the eyes. Retaliate first!' Jack asked a colleague, Sarah, about the 'eyes' and was told, 'Thomas was

(Continued)

(Continued)

exhorting you to develop the long, hard stare.' She sensed Jack's uncertainty and added, 'Face whatever comes in front of you with fortitude and stamina ... before long, eyes soften and become a twinkle.' Jack reflected and realised what they both were saying was he should exhibit a confident persona, remain steadfast and earn respect. Perhaps Jack needed the message put more simply – impress and you will be looked upon as impressive.

At the end of his first year, Jack was pleased with the way his lessons had been received and assessed; his interactions with staff and students had been positive; the contribution he had made to school projects and programmes was commented on with encouragement and gratitude; the progress in his personal and professional development was deemed good; the positive comments on his behaviour management boosted his self-esteem and generated a belief that he could and would do the job well; his health and general well-being had remained strong. He acknowledged the support from colleagues and, feeling more like an old hand, said he would advise two newly appointed teachers to work hard to make a good impression on everyone around them from what he called 'Day Zero' (the last day before his official start day).

Let's just reflect on what impressions of the school we create. Put yourself in the position of a new learner at the school. Here are some questions that will shape what they feel life is going to be like in the school:

- Can I find my way about the school?
- Is signage promising, i.e. creating a feeling that I'm wanted?
- If my first language is not English, are there translations of notices?
- Am I greeted with sincerity and a natural smile?
- Do I feel safe?
- Is there somewhere to wait and something to do whilst I wait to go into class?
- Can I see where the toilets are?
- Are other learners in the vicinity well behaved?

If you are happy with your answers to those questions then you will be happy and all around you will be happy. If anything goes wrong and you feel the impression created for the new learner is not what you wanted it to be, do not fear. You can sort it out quickly and then, with confidence and consistency, you will quickly rebuild the impression – if you do, this will become a lasting impression. If you don't, this will become a lasting impression, and we don't want this, do we?

Hot Tip: Never underestimate the power of an impression - impressions are not just flights of fancy but are real and can be worked on in relationships, interactions, creations, even with the most challenging learner. They can be made solid but they can also be reformed, changed and reborn.

2.5 KNOW WHAT APPROACHES YOU NEED TO WORK ON TO CONTROL YOUR STRESS LEVELS AND DEAL WITH CONFLICT IN THE CLASS

We have news for you! Conflict in the classroom is inevitable and you can deal with this in a *fight or flight* manner. If you fight, be wary of the victims. If you flee, be aware that you may only be putting things off. There are a number of books on the issue of stress or behaviour management, including Bill Rogers' excellent *Classroom Behaviour* (2015) and his concept of *relaxed vigilance*, that are well worth reading. Trying to condense all of the various writers' views on the subject into a simple blueprint for what you need to do to deal effectively with stress is virtually impossible, with each writer offering their own perspective on the subject. Never one to duck a challenge however, what follows are the 3 Rs, which you may want to work on and that we suggest underpin most of the stress management approaches that you will read about.

1. RELAX

All three of the authors of this book have recently rekindled a passion for playing football (of the walking variety). One of us read an article recently about a game down south between two teams where there had been a history of conflict. As the referee blew his whistle to start the game, both teams set about pushing and punching each other. Nothing too dire here (although they were all over the age of 60), until the referee grabbed one of the players and began thumping him. Quite clearly, the referee was caught up in the tenseness of the situation and reacted very badly.

As a teacher, you quite clearly can't afford to do this. Learning to relax during a classroom crisis or conflict situation is something that very few people master really well and is something that needs to be worked on. If you haven't found the approach you are looking for, here are two that might help:

(i) **Neuro-Linguistic Programming** (NLP) was developed in the early 1970s by Richard Bandler and John Grinder (1990) as a methodology to understand and change human behaviour patterns. The breakdown of the term defines what NLP is all about:

- **Neuro** is how you use your senses to make sense of what's happening, which in turn influences how you feel and what you say and do.
- **Linguistic** is the language and communication systems that you use to influence yourself and others.
- **Programming** is a succession of steps designed to achieve a particular outcome.

An NLP technique to conquer stress is to notice what triggers your stress reactions. When you can pick out these triggers, you can execute techniques to avoid them. If they are events that you have control over, then it is only a matter of changing or avoiding those triggers. If you don't have control over them, learning how to redirect your anxiety, worry and fear will cause a great increase in your well-being.

NLP uses a technique called *anchoring* to elicit the desired emotional responses to external stimuli. One way you can utilise this technique is to focus on a time you were incredibly relaxed. You need to make this memory as bright, vivid and lifelike as possible in your mind. Make this memory come to life as you feel the waves of relaxation wash over you. The key step is then to anchor it to an external stimulus. One way to do this is to try pushing your forefinger and thumb together on one hand. Focus on the intense feelings of relaxation as you complete the act of putting your fingers together. Do this several times in a row and practise it every day. Eventually, you will be able to link the act of pushing your fingers together to the feelings of relaxation that you imagined. Use this technique when you are feeling stressed in dealing with challenging behaviours.

(ii) **Mindfulness** is based on some of the principles of Buddhism. It was the work of Jon Kabat-Zinn in the 1990s that popularised it as a stress management tool. According to Kabat-Zinn (1994), *mindfulness* is about dealing with thoughts in a detached, de-centred and non-judgemental manner. Central to Kabat-Zinn's theory is the notion of using meditative techniques to stay in the body and to observe what thoughts are going on in the mind but not to identify with them. As well as a useful tool for parents and teachers, mindfulness can also be used to improve the learner or young person's ability to concentrate on tasks and to stay calm when things aren't going well. We realise that this might sound a bit abstract and complicated at first, but it isn't. Here's how you can do it, even with your busy teaching schedule:

- **Focus on your breathing**: find somewhere comfortable to sit and spend a few minutes doing nothing but breathing slowly in and out. Breathe in through one nostril, counting upwards from one to seven and then out through the other nostril counting downwards from seven to one. Repeat the process, starting with the other nostril. Focus all of your attention on your breath. When thoughts surface that distract you from your breathing, don't worry. Just let them pass, and shift your attention back to your breathing. After some practice, you should be able to spend a few minutes doing nothing but immersing yourself in the act of breathing, at the expense of all other thoughts.

- **Go for a walk**: instead of sitting in the staff room during tea break reflecting on what a bad morning you are having, go for a short walk. All you need to do is focus solely on the act of walking and the sensations of your surroundings (the cool breeze, the drizzle or the hot sun, or the dog barking in the distance). When you feel negative thoughts creeping into your mind, focus even harder on the sensation of walking. Focusing on something that's second nature is refreshing because it alters your frame of mind as you turn off the never-ending stream of negativity that has been dominating your attention.
- **Focus on the positive aspects of your life**: one of the main goals of mindfulness is to stop the stream of negative thoughts that arises when you feel that you are losing control. A great way to do this is to choose a short, positive message about yourself and repeat it over and over with each breath to keep your mind on track. The simplicity of this approach will keep you grounded in the exercise and stop negative thoughts from taking over.

Any moment when you feel stressed, overwhelmed or stuck on something is the perfect moment to practise whatever relaxing practices work for you. Just stop what you're doing, let the thoughts go for a moment and practise your favourite technique (anchoring, breathing, walking or positive self-talk). Even a few minutes of this can make a huge difference in quieting your mind and reducing stress. You'll be surprised how reasonable things look once you've taken a few moments to clear your head.

Most people accept that taking time over their hygiene (showering, brushing teeth, etc.) and exercising are essential but ignore the care and attention needed for their greatest asset – their mind. Gandhi was once with a group of followers who inquired about his schedule. He told them, 'I need to set aside at least one hour each day to meditate'. They were vexed by this and told him, 'We are busy men, there's no way that we have that much time to waste!'. Gandhi responded, 'Well, if that's the case, then you need to set aside two hours a day to meditate'.

> **Hot Tip**: The mind can be the source of happiness or despair, creativity or self-destruction, or problem-solving or problem-making. Look after it!

2. RESPOND

Between the three of us, we've taught all ages in all organisations: schools, colleges, universities, training centres, even prisons and bail hostels. It's very rare that conflict in any of our classes has resulted in violence but on one occasion that it did happen to one of us, our co-author had to act decisively. For what happened, see example 2.13.

Example 2.13: Act in haste; repent at leisure

Two trainee teachers (both women in their 50s) were arguing during a break in the session over use of the coffee-dispensing machine. One of the women grabbed the other by the throat and pushed her back. The incident was reported to the tutor. His default position was that violence was unacceptable and a risk to the health and safety of others. Excluding the perpetrator was the only solution. The individual was a third of the way through her teacher training programme and his decision almost certainly meant the end of her teaching career. He admits that he didn't like the woman: he felt that she was a bit odd and not popular with other learners. Excluding her went down well with the rest of the group and he confessed that he was pleased with himself for acting so assertively, as he had a tendency to avoid confrontation.

Our co-author realised some 20 years after the event that he may have acted instinctively and not been fair to the excluded individual. To be fair, you need to:

- gather as much information as you can about the circumstances that led to the conflict
- approach the situation in a calm and assertive manner
- listen to what all concerned in the conflict (observers as well as contributors) have to say
- make an assessment as to which approach to adopt
- set out the facts and explain why you have adopted the approach you have
- try to remain non-confrontational and focus on the issue, not the person.

No need to send us a postcard with your answer as to whether or not he was being fair. We're not sure if the end result would have been any different but, had he acted in line with the above, he may not have been questioning himself some 20 years later.

Kenneth Thomas and Ralph Kilmann (1974) suggested five approaches (avoid, compete, compromise, collaborate, accommodate) that can be used to respond to conflict between two parties. They argued that understanding the possible consequences of each approach will enable you to select which one to use. In the model in Figure 2.2, we have categorised approaches in terms of the likely win–lose outcome from the perspective of the teacher.

The consequences of each of the approaches from the teacher's perspective are:

	Teacher Wins	Teacher Loses
Learner Loses	Competing	Circumventing
	Conceding	
Learner Wins	Cooperating	Complying

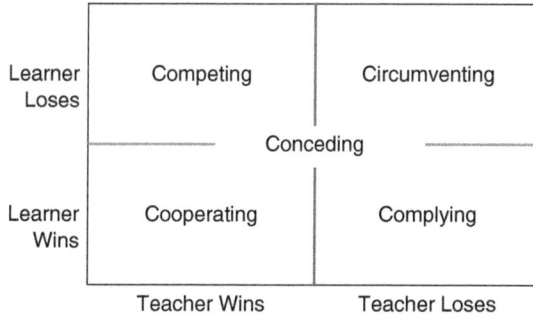

Figure 2.2   The 5 Cs win–lose conflict model

Source: Adapted from the Thomas-Kilmann Conflict Mode Instrument (1974)

- *Circumventing*: the teacher avoids dealing with conflict. In this case, both the teacher and learner lose.
- *Complying*: the teacher sacrifices their own needs to satisfy the needs of the learner. In this case, the learner wins and the teacher loses.
- *Conceding*: both parties agree to make concessions to the other person. In this case, both the teacher and the learner partially win/lose.
- *Competing*: the teacher satisfies their own needs at the expense of the learner. In this case, the teacher wins and the learner loses.
- *Cooperating*: both parties are being fully satisfied. In this case, both the teacher and the learner win.

Only if the teacher and the learner agree to cooperate will both parties be fully satisfied. Making concessions may result in both parties being partially satisfied. Acting in an aggressive (competing) or passive (conceding) manner may gain short-term results but will do little for long-term relationships. Avoiding dealing with conflict could have disastrous consequences for both the teacher and the learner.

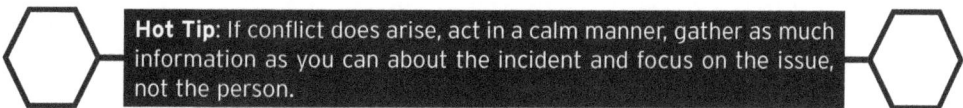

Hot Tip: If conflict does arise, act in a calm manner, gather as much information as you can about the incident and focus on the issue, not the person.

3. REFLECT

The terms reflection and critical reflection are becoming more popular in working practices, with many arguing that reflection is an essential aspect of the teacher's personal and professional development. What isn't clear from the literature is exactly what reflection entails. At one end of the spectrum, the emphasis is on reflection as a systematic, scientific approach (e.g. Aristotle and Dewey). At the other end, reflection deals with the implicit and the intuitive (Schön, 1983, 1987; Brookfield, 1995; Bolton, 2010). Both ends of the spectrum provoke questions relating to the scope, objectivity and quality of reflection. In this section, we want to focus on the implicit and intuitive reflective models that have more depth to them than the systematic and scientific approaches, and how they can be applied to teaching.

Donald Schön (1983, 1987) suggested ways in which teachers could become aware of their implicit knowledge and learn from their experiences both in and out of the classroom. Schön believed that reflection begins in working practices, particularly where the teacher is confronted with unique and conflicting experiences in the classroom – what Schön referred to as 'the swampy lowland messes'. He argued that it is from these experiences that teachers develop their own connections between the theory and practice which work for them.

Schön proposed two types of reflection:

- **Reflection-on-action**: this is after-the-event thinking whereby the teacher reviews, describes, analyses and evaluates past practice with a view to gaining insight to improve future practice.
- **Reflection-in-action**: this is thinking-whilst-doing whereby the teacher examines his/her own experiences and responses as they happen in the classroom. This is about them thinking on their feet and making snap decisions about what to do next.

Example 2.14: With experience can come wisdom

Sarah was a Spanish teacher who was asked to teach Spanish to a group of residents in a probation service bail hostel where there was zero tolerance for inappropriate behaviour. This was an experiment and a variation from the traditional literacy and numeracy classes that were being delivered in most offender institutions.

The experiment looked doomed to fail when Jim, an offender resident at the centre, refused to participate. Sarah told him *'Allí esta la puerta. Usala!'* When Jim asked what that meant, Sarah told him, 'There's the door, now use it!' Jim knew that Sarah meant business and that exclusion from the class might lead to him being returned to prison. Sarah also knew that if this happened, she might have to face repercussions from the other members of the group. Jim stayed and, by the third session, was helping some of the less-able learners with Spanish phrases.

Sarah's ability to assess the situation and think on her feet helped to avoid a potentially damaging situation for all concerned. Having the composure and confidence to handle a situation like this is something that takes time and effort to develop.

Although Schön argued that *reflecting-on-action* was important for teachers to gain insight to improve future practice, it was *reflecting-in-action* that he claimed was at the core of *professional artistry*, where practitioners develop the talent to *think-on-their-feet* and improvise. In both types of reflection, Schön suggested that practitioners seek to build new understandings that will shape their actions.

Stephen Brookfield (1995) argues that outstanding practitioners undergo a process of self-critical reflection whereby they constantly appraise their assumptions about their practice by seeing practice through four complementary lenses. It is through these lenses that the practitioner is able to access multiple, and distinctly different, vantage points from which to review practice.

Brookfield's critical lenses are the:

- **autobiographical** lens: this is where the teacher relates their experiences as a learner to reflect on what they are doing as a teacher
- **learner's** lens: this is where the teacher looks at themselves through their learners' eyes to reflect on whether they are interpreting their actions in the way they are intended
- **colleague's** lens: this is where the teacher uses their peers to help them reflect on hidden assumptions they may have about their practice
- **theoretical literature** lens: this is where the teacher undertakes research to make sense of, or question, their assumptions.

Brookfield argues that, in order to become critically reflective, using the lenses will produce a completely different picture of who we are and what we do. He is however cautious about the value of teachers sharing reflections with colleagues, claiming that public exposure of reflections that might indicate poor judgement can be damaging. He suggests that some teachers have a tendency to be self-effacing and feel unworthy of being part of the profession – what he refers to as the *imposter syndrome*.

Gillie Bolton (2010) argues that the working lives of teachers are stimulating, full of dilemmas, uncertainties and satisfactions. She talks about the futility of using mere reflection as an analytical tool and suggests that reflective practitioners need to adopt a *looking-through-the-mirror* approach which allows them to explore the wider, and rather perplexing, other side of the reflection. Her use of the analogy of Lewis Carroll's *Alice through the Looking Glass* makes Bolton's work one of the most interesting and enjoyable perspectives on the subject of reflection.

Bolton suggests that anyone journeying through the mirror will experience three paradoxes which are at the heart of reflection. These are:

- In order to acquire confidence, you have to let go of certainty.
- You get nowhere by looking for something when you don't know what it is.
- You achieve nothing by beginning to act when you don't know how you should act.

Bolton proposes that the results of facing up to these paradoxes are essential pre-requisites for reflective practitioners and will encourage teachers to have respect for and faith in themselves, to trust in the reflective process and recognise that uncertainty is vital for learning and change to take place.

The above represents three very powerful methods of reflection. Choose one, or any combination of the three, that works for you.

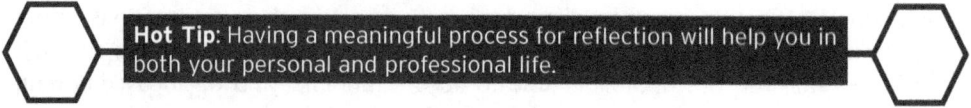

Hot Tip: Having a meaningful process for reflection will help you in both your personal and professional life.

2.6 KNOW WHO YOU CAN TURN TO FOR HELP

In the 2016 Bennett report *Developing Behaviour Management Content for Initial Teacher Training*, Bennett encourages Initial Teacher Training (ITT) providers to train or locate tutor guides, mentors and coaches with demonstrable abilities in behaviour management. He added that 'it is imperative that those training in behaviour management are taught by those with highly developed skills and understanding in this area' (p. 5).

In launching the Bennett report, Nick Gibb, the Minister of State for Schools, emphasised the critical role that school-based mentors should play in supporting teacher trainees to develop into effective teachers. He stated that 'this is particularly true as we continue to drive the move towards more school-led teacher training, as set out in the White Paper'.

It's important therefore to locate coaching and mentoring in respect of the various human resource development approaches that can take place in an organisation. A good starting point is to use the analogy of *learning to drive*:

- A **guide** will advise you on the most appropriate car to drive.
- A **mentor** will share their own driving experiences with you.
- A **coach** will encourage you to get in and drive the car correctly.

We'd like to take this one step further by introducing the notion of the critical friend into the equation. Arthur Costa and Bena Kallick describe a *critical friend* as 'a trusted person who asks provocative questions, provides a different perspective on an issue facing someone and critiques their actions with good intent' (1993: 50). Maybe someone fulfilling the role of a benevolent back-seat driver might fit in with the *learning to drive* analogy. Costa and Kallick outline a process for the critical friend–individual interaction in which the elements in the process can be summarised as:

- **Engagement**: You outline the problem and ask the critical friend for feedback.
- **Questioning**: The critical friend asks questions in order to understand the root causes of the problem and to clarify the context in which the problem is occurring.

- **Desired outcomes**: It is critical that you set the desired outcomes for the interaction, thus ensuring you are in control.
- **Feedback**: The critical friend provides feedback on what seems to be significant about the problem. This feedback should be more than a cursory look at the problem and should provide an alternative viewpoint that helps you address the problem.
- **Reflection**: Both you and the critical friend reflect on what was discussed.
- **Recording**: You record your views on the points and suggestions raised. The critical friend records the advice given and makes a note of what follow-up action they need to take.

Costa and Kallick argue that the notion of the critical friend is a very powerful idea, perhaps because it contains an inherent tension within the term; friends bringing a high degree of unconditional positive regard, whereas critics may be negative and intolerant of failure. They describe the ideal as a marriage of unconditional support and unconditional critique.

Example 2.15: Put the critical in critical friend

Ann was appointed Julie's mentor when she joined Ann's school as a newly qualified teacher. They had studied for their Certificates in Education at the same university and knew a lot of the tutors there. They quickly became friends.

Part of Ann's role as Julie's mentor was to observe her teaching. Ann would always congratulate Julie on her performance, describing aspects that were either very good or outstanding. Towards the end of Julie's probationary year, the school was Ofsteded.

Julie was devastated when the Ofsted inspector graded her performance 'Not adequate'. Ann tried to console her by saying how unfair the inspector had been and that Julie should complain about the grade. When Julie was observed by the school head, he confirmed the Ofsted inspector's assessment of Julie's inadequate teaching performance.

The role of the critical friend is a less formal approach than coaching or mentoring that can best be described as a professional undertaking based on mutual regard and willingness to question and challenge. Here are two important principles that underpin the relationship:

- Don't allow your friendship with the critical friend to obscure the real issue that you are faced with. Too much stress on the friendship side of the role may compromise the need for a deep and critical exchange of views. If they start sympathising with your plight, it will get you nowhere and it may even have a detrimental effect on coming up with a solution. The aim is for the critical friend to stimulate divergent thinking by introducing different views and fresh insights.

- Have a clear understanding of the boundaries that exist in the relationship and agree clear objectives of who will do what and by when. Make sure that you both review progress on the objectives at regular intervals. Encourage the critical friend to provide you with honest and critical feedback and be willing to accept this feedback. Finally, reflect on the nature and appropriateness of the relationship and ask whether this needs revising.

In Ann and Julie's case, Ann was quite clearly afraid that being critical of Julie's performance might have an adverse effect on their relationship. She wasn't secure either in her ability to act out the mentor's role or in their personal relationship.

Tom Bennett answered a number of challenging issues facing teachers in the classroom on the Times Educational Supplement (TES) website. He published a number of these in *The Behaviour Guru* (2010). This is a really good read that should be a must for all newly qualified teachers (NQTs) fighting their way through the swampy lowland messes they may encounter in the early years of their teaching careers (and probably well beyond that).

Hot Tip: Find someone (or something) who will support you in dealing with the more challenging behaviour that occurs in the classroom.

2.7 KNOW HOW TO SUPPORT LEARNERS WITH SPECIAL EDUCATIONAL NEEDS OR DISABILITIES

How inclusive or exclusive the teaching of children with additional needs should be is one of the most challenging questions in the education system. The question is challenging because, on the one hand, it requires clarity in how we characterise children and young people with additional needs and how this affects their behaviour and, on the other hand, there needs to be a thorough analysis of the appropriateness and effectiveness of the various approaches to teaching them. In *A Quick Guide to Special Needs and Disabilities* (2017), Bates uses the acronym TEACHERS to describe approaches that you can use when working with children and young people with special educational needs or disabilities who are exhibiting challenging behaviour in the classroom. These are:

- **T**alk to others. There is a potential army of people out there who can give you advice and support when working with a learner who has additional needs or disabilities.
- **E**ncourage the learner to be ambitious but realistic about what's achievable.
- **A**ccept that you won't get a quick fix when working with children with additional needs. Success usually comes in the form of a series of small gains, often achieved over a long period of time.
- **C**onsider the learner, not the disability. Adopt the philosophy that they are abled, but in a different way.
- **H**ave a positive approach to teaching children with disabilities.
- **E**mpathy, not sympathy, is required. Not all children want someone's pity; they may need help and support but, very often, sympathy is the last thing they want.
- **R**ealise that others have needs too. This includes you. Give the learner your best shot, but not at the exclusion of others in the class.
- **S**tress the importance of respect, both for oneself and others.

When normal tactics don't work with someone who has special needs, don't be afraid of entering their world. Example 2.16 involves someone who showed no fear in that respect.

Example 2.16: Getting the message across

Hope Adams is 11 years old. She was born with Down syndrome. She is a quiet, confident girl, well liked by everyone but, in common with most other 11-year-olds, prone to tantrums. When she goes *off on one*, she has to be told off and loses some of her classroom privileges. When this happens, she crunches the 2nd, 3rd and 4th fingers of her left hand into a fist and by raising the thumb and little finger makes an imaginary phone. She then 'punches' a few numbers into the 'phone' and tells her dad that her teacher, Mrs Smith, is being nasty to her. She then gives Mrs Smith a defiant look and warns her that her dad is going to 'sort her out'. In Hope's mind, this act gives legitimacy to her behaviour.

One day, after a particularly bad bout of tantrums and subsequent telling off by her teacher, Hope went to pick up her imaginary phone. As she did this, her teacher motioned to take it off her and, making her own 'phone', she told Hope's dad that Hope had been naughty and that he had to take the phone off her till her behaviour improved. Imagine Hope's look of amazement as this happened.

Mrs Smith could easily have used a real phone and told Mr Adams that Hope was behaving inappropriately. By entering Hope's world however, she was able to have a much greater impact on her behaviour than the consequences of a telling off from her parents would have.

> **Hot Tip**: Accept that you won't get a quick fix when working with children with additional needs. Success usually comes in the form of a series of small gains, often achieved over a long period of time.

2.8 KNOW HOW TO SUPPORT VICTIMS OF ABUSE

One of the most disturbing aspects of being a teacher is where the child that you are teaching is the victim of sexual abuse. Working with children and young people who are victims of sexual abuse is arguably one of the most distressing experiences for teachers. According to the National Society for the Prevention of Cruelty to Children (NSPCC):

- There are currently over 50,000 children in the UK who are identified as needing protection from abuse.
- This represents just 12.5% of the number of children who are being abused.
- One in 20 children in the UK has been sexually abused.
- One in three children who were sexually abused did not report the abuse.
- Over 90% of children who were abused were abused by someone they knew.
- Nearly 3,000 children were identified as needing protection from sexual abuse in 2014. (Bentley et al., 2016)

One of the sad aspects of children who are being sexually abused is that they feel they have done something wrong and that they are to blame. They often find silence is the only way to survive. Teachers have a major role to play in supporting children who may not have either the experience or the maturity to unravel the inner turmoil they face at being abused. By adopting a caring attitude and a willingness to listen, teachers will provide a trusting environment in which the learner will begin to recognise that they are capable and valued.

Example 2.17: Scarred for life

Brian was 9 years old and was on an overnight field trip when he was first sexually abused by someone who was a respected teacher, member of the church and family friend. The abuse continued after the trip with Brian and some friends being lured into the classroom storeroom for the abuser's gratification. Brian describes the fact that his feelings at the time were not one of repulsion at the abuser's acts but shame at the thought he was being naughty and deserved his punishment. He attributes keeping quiet for so long about the abuse to these feelings of shame and not wanting to hurt his parents.

Brian grew up to be a successful solicitor, a charismatic member of the England Grand Slam-winning rugby team in the 1990s and a television commentator. Few people who have seen Brian Moore (aka 'Pitbull') play rugby, and his aggressive and uncompromising style of play, would have associated him with the same man whose upsetting and heart-rending interview about the effects of his abuse on BBC News in 2013 helped to highlight the devastating effect that childhood abuse has on people.

For children and young people who are being abused at home, the classroom can be an environment which offers security and stability. Teaching staff, through their daily contact with the child or young person, have an opportunity to make a significant impact on their ability to deal with the abuse.

One form of sexual abuse that is causing concern, and often leading to children becoming withdrawn and not engaging in classroom activities, is female genital mutilation (FGM). FGM, also known as female circumcision or cutting, comprises all procedures involving partial or total removal of the external female genital organs. Like other forms of abuse, it is illegal in the UK and since 31 October 2015 there has been a statutory duty placed on teachers to report to the police any cases where they suspect FGM has taken place. There are nearly 140,000 reported cases of FGM in the UK with over 30 million girls worldwide being at risk of FGM over the next decade.

Example 2.18: Doubly scarred

Animatta lives in Burkina Faso, and like many girls where she lives she underwent FGM when she was 7 years old. 'I was scared', she says. 'Being cut is an event that I will never forget'. Animatta now has two daughters of her own and is determined not to let them suffer the same fate that she did. 'Deciding not to let my daughter get cut was a tough decision to make', she says. 'Going against tradition can be difficult. First you need to convince yourself that the decision you are making is the best one - you need to know the facts in order to do that. Only once you understand what FGM is and the consequences, can you make the courageous decision to go against tradition'. She concluded by saying: 'I hope my daughters will have a better life, better health because of my decision and I hope that they will do the same for their daughters'.

Evidence of FGM can either be visual signs or disclosure by the victim. It will be rare for teachers to see actual visual evidence of FGM but there may be tell-tale signs if the victim appears to be in discomfort when sitting for long periods, needing to make frequent trips to the toilet, becoming withdrawn and hesitant when having to change clothing for PE or dance class, or when talking about a painful ceremony they have experienced, especially following a visit to their country of origin.

Strategies for supporting a learner who has been sexually abused include the following:

- Recognise that they may have little self-esteem or lack a sense of identity.
- Support them to learn that they are valued and accepted and to see themselves as having something to contribute that others appreciate.
- Work with them to realise that it's not them who is to blame. Be aware that victims may often resort to silence, or be protective of the perpetrator, in an attempt to avoid action being taken against the abuser, especially if this involves close family members.
- Don't treat them any differently from other children and young people in the classroom or do anything that sets them apart from their peers.
- Respect and maintain their privacy. Unlike some physical impairments or psychological disorders where making others aware of their condition may be good for them, victims of abuse may not want this known to others.
- Refrain from touching them, especially if the abuse has been of a sexual nature, as this can give out the wrong message to them. Use other forms of encouragement such as nods and smiles.
- Keep a watchful eye on any health and well-being issues that they might be experiencing.
- Refer any suspicions you have about abuse to the proper authorities.
- Be prepared to listen to any problems they are having.

The NSPCC offers excellent advice on how to recognise the symptoms of abuse and how to deal with it on its website: learning.nspcc.org.uk/child-abuse-and-neglect/child-sexual-abuse.

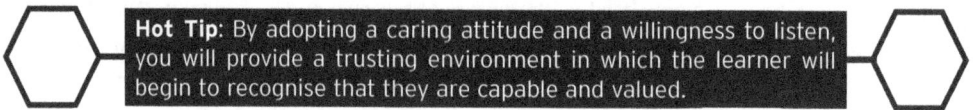

> **Hot Tip:** By adopting a caring attitude and a willingness to listen, you will provide a trusting environment in which the learner will begin to recognise that they are capable and valued.

2.9 KNOW HOW TO SUPPORT VICTIMS OF RADICALISATION

Extremism can take many forms, including political, religious and misogynistic extremism. Protecting children from any extremist views they may encounter, now or later in their lives, is arguably one of the most challenging issues facing education today.

The Department for Education's 2015 guide to schools and childcare providers, *The Prevent Duty*, explains what the duty means for schools and childcare providers. The guidance makes it clear what they should do to demonstrate compliance with the duty and informs them about other sources of information, advice and support. It does not stipulate that they need to have a dedicated Prevent policy. They should however have clear procedures in place for protecting children at risk of radicalisation, which may be set out in their existing safeguarding policies.

The following indicates, though not exclusively, that a student may be in danger of, or undergoing, the process of radicalisation:

- possessing and distributing extremist literature
- using extremist ideology to explain their personal disadvantage
- justifying the use of violence to solve societal issues
- boasting of joining extremist groups
- significant changes in their appearance and/or behaviour.

Most teachers are encouraged to undertake the same method of making a referral as they would if they had concerns regarding a safeguarding issue. The 5 Rs is a standard method of doing this:

- **Recognise**: Ask what signs of radicalisation are evident.
- **React**: Listen in to conversations between parties. Don't interfere. Don't ask leading questions.
- **Record**: Immediately record the detail of what you saw, overheard or witnessed.
- **Report**: Pass on the details immediately to the appropriate personnel. Do you know who they are?
- **Reflect**: Take time to reflect on the outcome of what happened. Ask yourself if it could have been handled differently.

Having policies and procedures in place is important but they often fail to capture the hearts and minds of children. Here is an approach developed by a theatre group, The Play House, in the West Midlands that attempts to do just that.

Tapestry is an interactive theatre performance and workshop programme originally designed and developed by The Play House in partnership with the West Midlands Counter Terrorist Unit (CTU) and Birmingham City Council (BCC) as part of the Prevent programme to challenge extremist ideology, as well as provide tools for participants to challenge it in a real-life situation. See the box for a summary of what Tapestry is about.

Tapestry

An opening montage of very short scenes was developed to illustrate the current context to the drama, making references to a range of incidents and issues, including 'lone wolf' Anders Brevik, ISIS, young people leaving the UK to fight in Syria, the

(Continued)

(Continued)

beheading of charity worker Alan Hemming, social media being used as a tool by extremists such as Britain First's technique of using popular and inoffensive-seeming posts on Facebook that click through to a right-wing extremist political organisation.

The performance is introduced by the narrator who explains the format of the session. They conduct a brief exercise to assess participants' attitudes by asking them to give a thumbs up or a thumbs down to indicate whether they agree with three statements: 'There is more that unites us than divides us'; 'I am allowed to say whatever I want, even if it offends you'; and 'If you want things to change, you have to be prepared to fight'.

For the drama, the three main characters are: (a) Hassan – a young Muslim man of Pakistani heritage who is becoming increasingly angry about the racism he experiences personally, and about negative attitudes to Muslims in general; (b) Jason – a young white man who is frustrated at being out of work and feels disaffected with life in general; and (c) Nazreen – a mixed-race Muslim woman who knows them both. Hassan and Jason have both been exposed to extremist ideology.

The performers have researched and prepared a back story for each of their characters so that they may refer to these during the hot-seating that follows the drama. This is where children are allowed to question each of the characters' behaviour.

Projects such as Tapestry, which focus on both extreme right-wing and Al Qaida-inspired ideology, provide participants with an opportunity to discuss the issues outlined in a fictional context that has been carefully constructed to ensure that they are able to express their views freely and challenge the views of others in a safe environment. Whilst contact with individual children is limited because their engagement is through a one-off session, its format means that the project can reach large numbers over a short space of time, addressing several different outcomes of the Prevent strategy.

Hot Tip: Having policies and procedures in place to deal with radicalisation is important but something more may be needed to capture the hearts and minds of children who are victims or perpetrators of radical behaviour.

SUMMARY OF PART 2

In Part 2, we have looked at a number of issues that affect your capacity to be a great teacher. We have also looked at how contemporary issues relating to additional needs, abuse and radicalisation are being addressed, and encouraged you to reflect on your default position and the qualities you need to work on to be more effective in dealing with challenging behaviour. Some key points to emerge from this are the following:

- Discuss with your learners which classroom rules you all feel comfortable with but have a small number of *given rules* such as non-threatening behaviour and respect for others' views that you are not willing to compromise on.
- Agree what are acceptable negative consequences (sanctions) for non-compliance with the rules. Agree what are acceptable positive consequences (rewards) for compliance with the rules.
- Write up the rules and give everyone (including your line management) a copy and/or display these in a prominent position. If anyone infringes the rules, make them aware that it is *their* rules they are breaking.
- Make sure that there are enough popular toys and resources and sufficient activities available so that children are meaningfully occupied without the need for unnecessary conflict over sharing and waiting for turns.
- Exercise restraint and avoid shouting or raising your voice in a threatening way to respond to children's inconsiderate behaviour. Never use physical punishment, such as smacking or shaking. Never send children out of the room by themselves or use a 'naughty' chair. Never threaten children with these. Only when there is a risk of physical injury to children or adults and/or serious damage to property should physical restraint, such as holding, be used.
- Teach learners to understand the outcomes of any inconsiderate action on their part and support them in learning how to cope more appropriately.
- Support each child in developing self-esteem, confidence and feelings of competence and in developing a sense of belonging in the group, so that they feel valued and welcome.
- Recognise and appreciate when the child displays considerate behaviour, such as kindness and a willingness to share, and avoid creating situations in which children receive adult attention only in return for inconsiderate behaviour.
- In cases of serious misbehaviour, such as racial or other abuse, make clear immediately the unacceptability of the behaviour and attitudes. Do this by means of explanations rather than by attributing personal blame.
- Recognise that the mind can be the source of happiness or despair, creativity or self-destruction, or problem-solving or problem-making. Look after it!
- When dealing with conflict, approach the situation in a calm and assertive manner, gather as much information as you can about the circumstances that have led to the conflict, listen to what all concerned in the conflict (observers as well as contributors) have to say, make an assessment as to which approach you need to adopt, set out the facts and explain why you have adopted the approach you have. Try to remain non-confrontational and focus on the issue, not the person.
- Having a meaningful process for reflection will help you in both your personal and professional life.

- Find someone (or something) who will support you in dealing with the more challenging behaviour that occurs in the classroom.
- When working with a learner with additional needs or disabilities, talk to others who can give you advice and support, encourage the learner to be ambitious but realistic about what's achievable, accept that you won't get a quick fix and that success usually comes in the form of a series of small gains, often achieved over a long period of time.
- As a teacher of learners with additional needs, you need to have the important qualities of patience and perseverance. It's important to consider the learner, not the disability, and to have a positive approach to teaching children with disabilities. Realise that others have needs too. This includes you. Give the learner your best shot, but not at the exclusion of others in the class.
- By adopting a caring attitude and a willingness to listen, you will provide a trusting environment in which the learner will begin to recognise that they are capable and valued.
- Be aware that having policies and procedures in place to deal with radicalisation is important but that something more may be needed to capture the hearts and minds of children who are victims or perpetrators of radical behaviour.

PART 3

DEALING WITH CHALLENGING INDIVIDUALS

In this part of the book, we want to look at the individuals who disrupt lessons and make your life a misery. They vary from the learners who are guilty of more serious forms of disruption such as violent or abusive behaviour, through the prolific and persistent offenders who cause regular minor disruptions, to learners who have an exaggerated sense of high or low self-worth. Their actions can be of an annoying or disturbing nature or a refusal to attend or participate in the lesson. The underlying causes can be of a neurological or psychological nature or simply a desire on their part to want to cause disruptions. An important aspect of managing the challenging behaviours that result from this is an understanding of what's causing the behaviour.

In each of the sections that follow, there are a number of real-life case studies, interspersed with some fictional extracts that serve to show the actions and characteristics of learners demonstrating challenging behaviour, and the impact that their behaviour had on the teacher concerned and the rest of the class. Each section then discusses approaches for dealing with the individuals and something to reflect on if you suspect that you may be displaying characteristics similar to the learners in section 3.1.

3.1 MAKING EVERYONE FEEL SAFE AND CONFIDENT

Protecting your learners from physical or psychological intimidation is arguably the most important role that you as a teacher can have. Intimidation can occur inadvertently, as a consequence of poorly thought-out actions or comments or as part of a planned process of coercion. In this section, we want to introduce you to a number of characters whose actions, intentional or unintentional, may threaten the well-being of other learners in the classroom and compromise your efforts to make your class a safe learning environment for your learners. The characters are:

a.   The **shell**: the learner who shows no remorse or guilt if they offend you or their classmates through inappropriate comments.
b.   The **rock**: the learner who displays a callous disregard and a lack of empathy for others who may not share their points of view.
c.   The **bully**: the learner who threatens or intimidates others.
d.   The **alpha type**: the learner who has to be leader of the pack and will use whatever powerhold they have over others to maintain their position.

THE SHELL

The *shell* is the learner who shows no remorse or guilt if they offend you or other learners through inappropriate comments. They vary from those who inadvertently offend others to those who have a malicious desire to want to hurt the feelings of others.

Example 3.1: Cut out name-calling

Jill was teaching a group of 14-year-olds when she heard one of the members of the class, Shelley, call a classmate and friend, Nicky, a 'bitch'. Jill asked Shelley 'why she had called her that'. Shelley just shrugged and said 'well, she is one'. The class started laughing (even Nicky). Jill asked if 'calling someone a female dog was nice'. Shelley was now on a roll and said, 'it's a compliment when you're as ugly as she is'. More laughter and Nicky now joined in with 'you need talk, you're like a monkey'. This gained a few 'Oohs' and 'aahs' from the class. Shelley was African English and stared menacingly at Nicky. Jill tried to regain control of the class and, although the name calling had ended, the tension between Shelley and Nicky was noticeable.

Jill now has a difficult issue to deal with. Shelley's name calling was unfortunate and uncalled for. The word 'bitch' however is fairly common parlance in street culture. Jill had to decide whether Nicky's use of 'monkey' was also unfortunate and uncalled for or said with racist intent. Jill decided not to make a formal record of events but asked Shelley and Nicky to stay behind after class. She asked the two girls, 'what was that all about?' Both looked sheepishly at each other and said 'sorry'.

Unfortunately, this wasn't the end of the matter and, the following day, Shelley's parents complained to the head teacher as this wasn't the first time their daughter had been the subject of a racist slur.

Name calling has almost become an accepted part of school culture. There will be some members of the class who don't feel 'part of the gang' unless they have a nickname. Each of us remembers the nicknames that were given to our teachers and classmates (including our own – wouldn't you like to know!). Some were quite innocent and inoffensive whereas others were cruel and insensitive. Mocking people by giving them nicknames based on their physical characteristics, disabilities, race or religion is unacceptable and may have long-term consequences for people. For example, Richard, one of our classmates, had diabetes and his nickname 'Sugar' stayed with him well into his adult life.

The difficulty is how to stop people making inappropriate comments or name calling. Making the *shell* aware of the negative impact they are having on someone by the inappropriateness of their comments will only work if the *shell* is capable of remorse. The *shell* may also be incapable of empathising with others, so asking them how they would feel if they were called something cruel may be fruitless.

Strategies for dealing with *shells* include:

- Don't try to get them to empathise. Never ask them how they would feel if they were called something that highlighted a physical or cultural characteristic.
- Have appropriate ground rules. Build a 'no offensive name calling' policy into your classroom ground rules.
- Keep a record of incidents of name calling. If this is being done in a malicious and persistent manner then come down on it with all the force you can muster.
- Report any incidents where you suspect the name calling infringes anti-discriminatory laws.

We would hope that, as a teacher, you never intentionally call someone by their nickname. Even if this appears inoffensive to you, you may not be aware of the effect it has on the individual, or you could be accused of showing favouritism towards them if you do. Try to imagine how difficult it is to impose sanctions on someone who you refer to affectionately by their nickname. The use of inappropriate comments goes beyond using nicknames and you may have opinions relating to someone's religious or cultural beliefs that you just can't resist talking to them about. We know that classroom discussion and debate over current issues is important but there are occasions when it's better for you to keep your views to yourself for fear of offending someone.

THE ROCK

The *rock* is the learner who displays callousness and a lack of empathy towards other children who may not share their points of view. This could be as a result of a stubborn belief in something or a complete refusal to acknowledge that the other person is allowed to have an alternative point of view.

Example 3.2: His own worst enemy, but only just

Dwayne was a strongly opinionated 15-year-old who could quite literally have an argument with himself in a coffin. His extreme views on most subjects – sport, music, religion, etc. – made him an easy target for anyone looking for a fight.

This backfired badly on him when a group of opposing football fans were talking about how much better their team was than Dwayne's; the other boys' arch rivals. Not accepting they were bigger, older and greater in number than he was, Dwayne couldn't resist telling them they were talking nonsense (he used stronger words than this).

The other boys just smiled. Instead of making his point and retreating gracefully, Dwayne took it on himself to start telling the other boys about his team's proud record and how their team were c**p by comparison. The more the other boys smiled, the more aggressive Dwayne grew and the more expletive his language became. Not willing to take any more from him, one of the other boys pushed Dwayne to the ground.

Classroom debates can be great fun and a useful learning experience. The *rock* is different from the classroom bully, who intimidates classmates into agreeing with them through their physical or intellectual superiority, because the *rock* may be lacking in both respects. What they do have is a stubborn refusal to back down and an unshakeable belief that they are right.

Leon Festinger (1957) spearheaded the social psychology movement in the USA. He suggested that people continually seek to bring order or meaning to their beliefs by developing routines and opinions that may give rise to irrational and sometimes maladaptive behaviour. He claimed that when these routines are disrupted, or opinions are contradicted, the individual starts to feel uncomfortable: a state that Festinger referred to as *cognitive dissonance* (aka discord in reasoning). Festinger argued that cognitive dissonance makes someone of strong conviction unlikely to change their opinion, even if they are presented with a rational argument to the contrary.

Festinger was inspired to study people's unshakeable conviction in their beliefs when he read an article about a cult whose members believed the Earth was going to be destroyed by floods. When the anticipated apocalypse didn't materialise, committed cult members, who had given up their homes and jobs, convinced themselves that it was due to their dedication and sacrifice that the world was spared.

You are unlikely to be faced with individuals whose beliefs are as radical as the cult that Festinger studied, but you need to be wary that there will be some *rocks*, like Dwayne, whose convictions are that strong that they will be resistant to any disagreement with their arguments. Trying to get them to act in a way that is inconsistent with their beliefs or convictions is likely to cause cognitive dissonance.

Strategies for dealing with *rocks* include:

- Don't try to force them to change their beliefs. Forcing someone to change their beliefs may not be feasible or even acceptable. Making them feel bad or guilty about their actions is not a great way of teaching someone and may cause even greater cognitive dissonance.
- Get them to reflect. Trying to get an individual to think about their actions in a different manner or context so that it no longer appears to be inconsistent with their beliefs, is an approach worth considering. Do this and dissonance is less likely.
- Avoid trying to get individuals to learn by challenging their firmly held beliefs on a subject, even if you consider that belief to be inappropriate. Who is to say that your beliefs are any more valid than theirs?
- Don't think that change is inevitable. Accept that, despite your best efforts, there are some learners who will never change their ideas or ways of doing things.
- Reflect on your actions. Question whether it is your right to try to change their ways.

We suspect that there are some teachers who feel it demeans their position if they back down in a debate. *Shells* are people who make inappropriate comments, whereas *rocks* make appropriate comments; it's just their stubborn refusal to back down on an issue that causes problems.

THE BULLY

The *bully* is the learner who has poor control over their behaviour and intentionally torments others in physical, verbal or psychological ways. This can range from punching or shoving to threatening, name calling or mocking someone. This can be done face to face, through spreading malicious rumours or via social media. The consequences of bullying can vary from the victim being annoyed or feeling intimidated to something far worse.

Example 3.3: A life lost – blighting the lives of others

Tom was a teenage boy who lived with his parents in Birmingham. Tom was severely bullied in school. He became isolated and reliant on social media as his means of communicating with others. When, as a result of cyber-bullying, the bullying continued into his home, it became too much for Tom and, at the age of just 15, he committed suicide.

Tom isn't the only young person to be a victim of cyber-bullying. The rapid development of new technologies and the widespread access to them have provided a new medium for entering the private lives of people and have created a potentially bigger audience for virtual bullies.

One of the most distressing aspects of the *bully*'s behaviour is that it can be cruel and relentless. Like it or not, part of growing up involves teasing and being teased. Most children and young people will accept occasional bouts of this but, when it continues, they will experience distress and their health and education will suffer. Although bullying isn't the only cause of emotional distress, it remains an evil that everyone should work towards eradicating.

Lawrence Kohlberg (1973) argues that the need to bully, and to a lesser degree name calling and a lack of empathy, can be linked to a delay in the moral development of the bully. In his work, he tracks an individual's level of moral reasoning by assigning them to one of three levels, each encompassing two stages, making six stages in all. These are summarised as:

- **The Pre-conventional Level**: this level of moral thinking is that which is generally found at primary school level:

    i.   The first stage of this level is where children are deterred from bullying because they are told to do so by some authority figure (e.g. parent or teacher). This obedience is compelled by the threat or application of punishment.
    ii. The second stage of this level is characterised by a view that not being a bully means acting in one's own best interests.

- **The Conventional Level**: this level of moral thinking is that which generally starts in adolescence and continues into early adulthood:

    i.   The first stage of this level is characterised by an attitude in which young people refrain from bullying others to gain the approval of others.
    ii. The second stage is one oriented to abiding by the law and responding to the obligation of duty not to bully.

- **The Post-conventional Level**: this level of moral thinking is one that starts with adulthood but one which Kohlberg felt is not reached by the majority of adults:

    i.   The first stage of this level is where people develop an understanding of social mutuality and a genuine interest in the welfare of those being bullied.
    ii. The second stage is based on respect for the universal moral principle that bullying is wrong and on the demands of an individual's conscience.

Kohlberg believed that individuals could only progress through these stages one stage at a time; that is, they could not jump stages and could only come to an understanding of a moral rationale one stage above their own.

According to Kohlberg, it was important to present students with moral dilemmas for discussion which would help them to see the reasonableness of a 'higher stage' morality and encourage their development in that direction. One example that Kohlberg used was the 'Heinz Steals the Drug' scenario. In this, a woman has terminal cancer and her doctors believe that only one drug might save her. This drug had been discovered by a local pharmacist who was able to make it for $200 per dose and sell it for $2,000 per dose. The woman's husband, Heinz, could only raise $1,000 to buy the drug. He tried to negotiate with the pharmacist for a lower price or for extended credit to pay for it over time. The pharmacist refused to sell it for any less than the retail price or to accept partial payments. Rebuffed and desperate, Heinz instead broke into the pharmacy and stole the drug to save his wife. Kohlberg asked, 'Should the husband have done that?'

Kohlberg was not interested so much in the answer to the question of whether students considered Heinz to be right or wrong but in the reasoning for each student's response. In this respect, he believed that morality is not something that can be imposed on children but is developed through their interaction with others. As an educator, consider where your students' moral development lies in terms of Kohlberg's six stages:

- **Stage 1**: They know that if they bully someone they will be punished.
- **Stage 2**: They know that if they refrain from bullying they will be rewarded.
- **Stage 3**: They know that people will like them if they do something good for others.
- **Stage 4**: They know that it is important to respect authority and follow the rules on bullying.
- **Stage 5**: They understand the importance of considering the various opinions and values of other people before deciding on the morality of their action.
- **Stage 6**: They appreciate the need to allow their own conscience to be the ultimate judge of what's right and what's wrong.

If you are going to use Kohlberg's approach to moral development, think about how you could adapt his 'Heinz Steals the Drug' scenario to suit a teaching/learning situation relating to bullying.

It's important to take bullying seriously and not just brush it off as something that kids have to 'tough out'. The effects can be serious and affect kids' sense of safety and self-worth. In severe cases, bullying has contributed to tragedies such as suicide. There is however no legal definition of bullying. Defining bullying is left to your school and there should be a school policy statement that defines bullying and the action to be taken to prevent it happening.

Strategies for dealing with *bullies* include:

- Take bullying seriously. Make sure that the learners in your class understand that you will not tolerate bullying in any shape or form.
- Establish rules about bullying and stick to them. If you punish learners by taking away privileges, be sure it's meaningful.
- Teach all of your learners to treat others with respect and kindness. Teach them that it is wrong to ridicule others because they are different, for example as a result of their race, religion, appearance, special needs, gender or economic status.
- Try to instil a sense of respect for those who are different. Consider getting involved together in a community group where your learners can interact with people who are different.

- Try to understand what's causing the bully's behaviour. Talk with the parents of the bully, other teachers or guidance counsellors to look for insight into the factors that may be influencing them to act the way they are. Try to appreciate the kind of pressures they might be under at school or home that may be provoking their intimidating behaviour.
- Encourage good behaviour. Positive reinforcement can be more powerful than negative discipline. Catch the bully out being good to others and praise them for it.
- Be a good role model. Think carefully about how you talk in class and how you handle conflict and problems. If you behave aggressively towards learners in class, the chances are they'll follow your example.
- Make sure there is a school-wide code of conduct that reinforces school values and clearly defines unacceptable behaviour and the consequences of this happening.
- Build bullying prevention activities into teaching sessions through communication campaigns or creative arts activities, highlighting school values and reinforcing the message that bullying is wrong.
- Never tell someone who is being bullied to fight back. Often, victimised individuals really are weaker and smaller than the bully. Fighting back may therefore be the worst defence.
- Don't expect victims to work it out on their own. Bullying is not simply a problem of individuals; it is extremely unrealistic therefore to expect victims to alter the dynamics of bullying by themselves.

Teachers have a crucial role to play in the eradication of bullying. Any time teachers do not intervene, they are giving legitimacy to the act. They also have a role to play in modelling good behaviour in this respect.

Example 3.4: Bullies come in all shapes and sizes

One of us has clear memories of their first year of A level studies at school when they were asked to referee a football match between the staff and the fifth-formers. This was a reward for the fifth-formers winning the town's school soccer trophy. With the staff losing 3-0 and only ten minutes of the game to go, a member of the staff team deliberately kicks an opponent. Wow! Now there's a problem. What should the referee do? Obviously claiming that he'd never seen the incident was the sensible thing to do. Unfortunately, he doesn't do sensible and sent the offender off. It is 50 years later and he still has the clearest of recollections of passing the offending member of staff in the school assembly hall the following day and the teacher threatening him by saying that 'he'd have him if he came anywhere near him for the rest of the term'. Luckily, he wasn't a pupil in this particular teacher's class and there were only a few days to the end of the school year. He managed to survive this particular bully who was using his position as a teacher to intimidate him.

THE ALPHA TYPE

The *alpha type* is the learner who has to be leader of the pack and will use whatever powerhold they have over others to maintain their position. Let's look at a piece of literary genius to understand more about *alpha types*.

LORD OF THE FLIES

William Golding's *Lord of the Flies*, written in 1954, is the story of a group of boys stranded on a deserted island after their plane crashes. With no adult survivors to offer them guidance, they are left to fend for themselves and create their own 'micro-society'. Ralph is elected 'chief' and Jack is in charge of hunting for food. A bitter rivalry develops between Ralph and Jack as both want to take charge of the group. As Ralph tries to keep his group civilised, Jack's hunters become savage and primal. The growing hostility between Ralph and Jack leads to a bloody and frightening climax.

It's unlikely that you will encounter such bloody feuds in the class that happened in *Lord of the Flies*. Nevertheless, there will be power struggles that you need to be aware of and, more importantly, know how to deal with. To help you with this, you need first of all to understand the nature of power. There is a static and unilateral argument that power is something that some learners exert over their peers. To examine this further, we need to look at the different dimensions of power.

There are numerous models of power (see the earlier reference to Max Weber). One of the most compelling models was outlined by John French and Bertram Raven (1959). They identified five sources of power that an *alpha type* can call upon to encourage or compel compliance from their followers. These are:

- **positional power**: where the individual holds a position of authority
- **reward power**: where the individual has control over rewards that followers may cherish
- **coercive power**: where the individual has the physical or mental presence to force people to follow them
- **expert power**: where the individual has knowledge or expertise that impresses followers
- **charismatic power**: where the individual has the type of personality that others admire.

Strategies for dealing with *alpha types* include the following:

- Let them know who is in charge. As a teacher, you hold a position of authority over the *alpha types* in the class. Don't exceed the limits of that authority but don't allow them to subvert it either.
- Expect compliance and enforce it. Act with confidence when you exercise authority and expect the *alpha type* to comply with your legitimate requests.
- Use positive reinforcement. Identify the range of rewards you have control over. If you promise rewards on compliance, always deliver on any promises you make.
- Never use coercive power to force compliance with your demands. Trying to beat the *alpha type* at their own game is a dangerous tactic. Even if you do win, the long-term damage this may create in terms of your relationship with the *alpha type* or their followers may prove irreparable.
- Never complain to them that their actions are causing a disruption. They may see this as weakness in you and something they can exploit.
- Avoid challenging them to defend their positions. Instead, ask the *alpha type* to explain them.

We think it's fair that if we've used one piece of literary genius to portray *alpha-type* learners, we can use another piece to portray *alpha-type* teachers, or head teachers to be precise.

MATILDA

In Roald Dahl's book *Matlida* (1988), Matilda is a pupil at Crunchem Hall Primary School. Agatha Trunchbull is the fictional headmistress of the school. She is depicted as being a brawny, muscular woman serving as the remorseless headmistress of Matilda's school and is feared by pupils and staff alike. She is notorious for her wildly excessive and idiosyncratic alpha-type behaviour, such as demonstrating her Olympic hammer-throwing skills by hurling a girl over the fence and into a neighbouring field.

Miss Trunchbull is certainly not the sort of alpha type that you'd expect to find as headmistress of a school. Her treatment of her pupils, from force-feeding them cake to throwing them across the playground by their pigtails, is outrageous (yes, we know it's only a story!). It's for this very reason that she gets away with it as, according to Matilda, 'No parent is going to believe this pigtail story, not in a million years'.

3.2 DEALING WITH LOW-LEVEL DISRUPTORS

The majority of disruptions that occur in your classroom will be of a minor nature. You have to decide if it is worth stopping what you are doing to deal with it.

Sue Cowley (2010) argues that it is the frequency and nature of low-level incidents of misbehaviour that cause much of the stress in teaching, as minor disruptions frequently build into more troublesome ones. Therefore, they need to be addressed with the least amount of disruption to the class.

In this section, we want to introduce you to a number of characters whose actions, intentional or unintentional, may be a frequent annoyance to you or others and may disrupt your efforts to maintain classroom control.

The characters are:

a. The **fidgeter**: the learner who demonstrates abnormal and restless activity.
b. The **wind-up**: the learner who can't resist making practical jokes.
c. The **joker**: the learner who constantly fools around and tries to amuse others with their use of humour.
d. The **pop artist**: the learner who acts impulsively and irresponsibly in a persistent or prolific manner, causing disharmony within the class.
e. The **plagiarist**: the learner who lives off the knowledge and skills of their classmates and falsely claims credit for others' ideas.
f. The **deflector**: the learner who fails to accept responsibility for their own actions and tries to blame others when things go wrong.
g. The **narcissist**: the learner who is self-absorbed and only concerned with their own self-happiness.

THE FIDGETER

The *fidgeter* is the learner who just can't sit still. This isn't about the one occasion which may be due to the learner experiencing problems with seating or clothing or some form of physical discomfort, but about the learner whose persistent and prolific restlessness is causing distraction or disruption in the classroom. It's quite possible that although this may seem one of the less concerning of the examples of challenging behaviour, there may be mitigating circumstances, such as early signs of conditions such as Attention Deficit Hyperactivity Disorder (ADHD), that could easily elevate this to the top of the list of concerns.

> ## Example 3.5: Know the child to teach them well
>
> Jimmy is 10 years old, has ADHD and was having a bad day in his maths class. He liked maths because he saw something magical in numbers. His favourite was the 9 times table because when you added up the digits in the table they always equalled 9. He had already been told off in the lesson because he couldn't stop fidgeting in his seat.
>
> *(Continued)*

(Continued)

The school has a yellow card system where cautions are given for misbehaviour, with two yellows resulting in a red card and subsequent loss of *gold dust time* (play time). Jimmy had received a yellow card for leaving his seat during a group activity to look at what another group was doing.

When the teacher called on the groups to give their answers, Jimmy jumped up, shooting his hand up in the air, desperate to get the answer out. His teacher ignored him and asked another learner to give them their answer. Jimmy slumped back in his chair, disappointed at not being called upon to give his answer. After three children had given the wrong answer, Jimmy's teacher asked him if he knew the answer to the question. Jimmy started squirming in his seat and asked the teacher 'what question?'. For Jimmy, the moment had passed. He knew the correct answer and was frustrated at not being given the opportunity to show this to his teacher and peers. When others in the class laughed at his response, Jimmy lost even more of the little self-esteem he had and his fidgeting became even more frenetic.

The medical condition that is now known as ADHD was first proposed by UK paediatrician George Still in 1902. Until recently, it was referred to as *hyperkinetic disorder*. In 1994, the American Psychiatric Association (APA) categorised ADHD by behavioural characteristics such as inattention and/or impulsiveness. According to the APA, one of the conditions, known as Hyperactive Impulsive Type, is where the learner or young person may be seen fidgeting with their hands or feet, squirming in their seat or getting out of their seat and walking around the classroom at times when remaining seated is expected. As well as fidgeting, they may also have a tendency to be impatient and blurt out answers before questions have been completed. It is estimated that approximately 5% of school-aged children in the UK have some form of ADHD, with boys outnumbering girls by a ratio of 3:1.

In example 3.5, Jimmy's teacher has a bit of a dilemma. He wants to give Jimmy the opportunity to answer the question but can't allow Jimmy to answer all of the questions. Ignoring Jimmy however was wrong: he should have acknowledged Jimmy's efforts but explained that he wanted to give others a chance first.

If you recognise that a learner may be displaying signs of ADHD or a similar neurological condition then:

- Make sure that you are knowledgeable about the condition. Accept the legitimacy of the disorder but have a set of behavioural rules that both you and the individual sign up to.
- When setting rules, know when frustration levels (including yours) are rising and when it may be appropriate to back off slightly.

- Have a range of teaching strategies and materials that cater for the learning styles, abilities and skills of those with neurological conditions.
- Set clear achievement targets both for work and behaviour. Make it clear what the consequences are for failing to achieve these targets, but praise the individual immediately when they achieve a set target.
- Never ignore, ridicule or be openly critical of the learner.
- Seat the learner near to your desk with their back to the rest of the class to keep them from being distracted by others in the class, and avoid other distractions such as views and noise from windows and doors.
- Surround the learner with good role models and encourage them to participate in peer tutoring and cooperative learning.
- Have a private signal system (something as simple as a raised eyebrow or a tilt of the head may suffice) with them to let them know when you think they are acting inappropriately.

THE WIND-UP

The *wind-up* or *wind-up merchant* is the learner who *just cannot* resist playing practical jokes on people. Their jokes can vary from being extremely funny to being downright dangerous and harmful. Most wind-ups are not done with malicious intent but unfortunately on occasions they do backfire. The repercussions of this can be a fall-out in relationships or worse.

Example 3.6: Actions have consequences

Natalie was a great practical joker - great for some people but not so great for some of the victims! When Natalie was at college, knowing a fellow student had downloaded some material they had used in an assignment, she phoned them, pretending to be the principal's secretary, inviting the student to attend a plagiarism meeting. The student dashed out to meet with his tutor and confessed to what he had done. He wasn't amused by the 'gotcha' message that he heard on his answerphone when he returned.

We don't think that, like most practical jokers, Natalie intended to cause any distress and she was usually forgiven by her victims, although it was some time later for her college victim. It could be argued that the college student, by admitting he was at fault, was able to rescue a situation that may have had more serious repercussions had he not confessed and instead been caught out. Not all wind-ups work out quite as well.

Example 3.7: A game with consequences

A group of Year 12 pupils were having a crafty cigarette behind the bike sheds (don't tell me that you've never heard of this practice) when Georgie, a Year 10 pupil, came running round the corner shouting 'watch out, the head's coming'. The boys quickly dropped their cigarettes and ran. They were not amused when they found out the head wasn't there. The following week saw the same boys and the same situation. This time they told Georgie to 'get lost'. 'No honestly, he is coming', Georgie said. The smokers looked at each other and gave that 'can we really risk it?' look, before dropping their cigarettes and running. Again, they realised they had been the victims of Georgie's wind-up. OK, you've guessed what's coming; the following week and the same boys, same situation. This time they ignored Georgie's warning only to see an angry looking head teacher staring at them. Georgie made sure he avoided the ex-smokers for the rest of the term.

This of course is a variation of Aesop's fable about the *Boy that Cried Wolf,* that, when you read about the *procrastinator* later in the book, you will know is indelibly printed on one of the author's brains and should serve as a deterrent to any would-be wind-up merchant.

Strategies for dealing with the *wind-up merchant* include:

- Unless someone is hurt by the wind-up, allow them some latitude with the first one but let them know you won't tolerate them doing it again.
- If you are the victim of the wind-up, and you think it's appropriate to do so, play along with them as if you thought they were telling the truth. Let them see the consequences of their actions.
- Show them that you don't appreciate their humour but don't be too harsh on them when you do this.
- Accept that humour can have a place in the classroom, providing it isn't offensive or abusive.

Example 3.8 is an instance of how teachers who are wind-up merchants can get it horribly wrong.

Example 3.8: Stick to the facts

Criterion referencing is where a learner's work is assessed against set criteria. Norm referencing is where, regardless of the standard of work produced, only a percentage of learners will be awarded a pass mark. Levels, and some professional standards, are judged using norm-based referencing. A teacher-trainer once wound up a group of five trainee teachers by telling them that their course was assessed using norm-based referencing and that only 80% of the group would be allowed to pass. When two trainees who were close friends didn't turn up the following week, fearing that one of them would fail the course, he had to ring them up to explain that he was only winding them up. Needless to say, they were not happy and he learned his lesson from this.

Please don't be an idiot like one of us was in example 3.8. Most learners will appreciate a bit of light-heartedness from a teacher but they don't like being victims of a wind-up.

THE JOKER

The *joker* is the learner who constantly fools around and tries to amuse others with their use of humour. *Jokers* vary from the happy-go-lucky classroom prankster who classmates like to be around, to the annoying individual who has an over-inflated belief that they are funny and a mistaken belief that their role in life is to try to make others laugh.

Example 3.9: Just imagine

John was a self-confessed prankster and troublemaker: the type of person who, on his own admission, other children were told was a bad influence and to keep away from him. There was, however, something charismatic about John that drew others to him. This charisma had masked a number of problems John had faced in his childhood. His mother and father had separated when John was only 5 years old and throughout the rest of his childhood and adolescence he lived with his uncle and aunt. Although this made him envious and resentful of those children who had stable family lives, John learned some valuable skills from his uncle and aunt, such as story writing and how to play the mouth organ and banjo, during this time.

School reports would often describe John as 'a happy-go-lucky, good-humoured and lively lad with limited ability, who was certainly going to be a failure in life'. He lived up to these comments by failing all of his GCE O level exams. Despite this, he was accepted at a local art college, but was expelled before his final year because he never took his studies seriously. His premature death before his 40th birthday, at the hands of the murderer Mark Chapman, ended the career of arguably the greatest singer-songwriter the world has ever known.

Like John Lennon, one of us admits he was a bit of a joker at school. When he was in his 40s, he met an old schoolmate who told him that his humour and jokes took a lot of the tension out of exam time and helped relax her and a lot of others. The downside however was when ten years earlier and training to be a counsellor of people with disabilities, his trainer took him to one side after the first week of training and asked him why he was such a smart alec. He told him how annoying he found his humour and that it was undermining his control of the group.

Some 35 years after this encounter with his trainer, he often reflects on the appropriateness of his behaviour. He knows that acting the fool masked inadequacies in his own ability. He felt that he would always have a ready group of followers if he could make people laugh. This was OK, providing it didn't undermine the ability of others to teach and learn within the class.

John's story typifies the frustration you will feel in teaching the classroom *jokers*. They usually have a great line in put downs. You may be onto a loser if you try to compete with them. You can't however allow the put downs to undermine you as the class teacher. Sometimes a quizzical look (a sort of 'I don't understand that joke' look) or a shrug of the shoulders will suffice. There is nothing a joker hates worse than people not appreciating their humour. You must appreciate however that sometimes their humour is masking inadequacies they may be experiencing and a cruel put down of them could have serious consequences for both you and the *joker*.

Strategies for dealing with *jokers* include the following:

- Don't try to compete with them.
- Don't be a victim of their jokes.
- Show them that you don't appreciate their humour but don't be too harsh on them when you do this.
- Accept that humour can have a place in the classroom, providing it isn't offensive or abusive.
- Think about the appropriateness of your own use of humour.

Providing it doesn't prove too disruptive, most lessons can benefit from a bit of humour from the teacher.

Example 3.10: His days were numbered

When one of us studied for their maths degree in the late '60s, their quantum mechanics lecturer believed he could liven up what he clearly thought was going to be a boring session with a joke. At first, this was a bit of a novelty and most of the class laughed at his jokes. He quite clearly had a limited repertoire and, by the end of the first term, the laughter had turned to groans. He never quite believed that most of the class felt his subject was a fascinating part of the mathematics course and that he didn't need the distraction of telling jokes. Statistics, on the other hand, would have been less tedious with a few jokes thrown in.

THE POP ARTIST

The *pop artist* is the persistent or prolific (pop) offender who frequently acts in an impulsive and irresponsible manner and causes disharmony within the class. This can vary from children who just don't think before acting, to children with a serious neurological condition. Example 3.11 tells the tale of what one of us experienced just a couple of years ago.

Example 3.11: Listen to this

We first met Megan when she was 11 years old. We were visiting her school to observe and assess one of her teachers, Carrie. Throughout the lesson, Megan kept interrupting Carrie with stories about her favourite boy band. She even started singing songs by the band. At first, Carrie and the rest of the class, knowing all about Megan's behaviour, indulged her, but when this started to become disruptive Carrie gently motioned to her to be quiet. Megan reacted by folding her arms, slumping over her desk and refusing to participate in the lesson. This lasted for about five minutes, at which stage Megan turned her attention to the observer and hit him with a barrage of questions. Despite his polite refusal to respond, she said, 'you're nice, can I come home with you?'. We think at this point her teacher would have gladly allowed her to do this.

Although Megan was very sociable, she also had difficulty establishing long-term peer friendships and became anxious and over-reacted to the least thing. Like most disrupters, she talked enthusiastically about her favourite subjects but had a poor awareness of general conversational skills. Megan was later diagnosed as having William's syndrome, a condition caused by an abnormality in chromosomes that is characterised by a distinctive facial appearance (elfin-like) and a unique personality that combines over-friendliness with high levels of empathy and anxiety.

There doesn't have to be a neurological condition for disruption in the classroom to take place. If however this occurs in a prolific and persistent manner then it may be worth analysing the cause. Whilst dealing with classroom disruptions can be a challenge, it is important to remember that, in many cases, the *pop artists* inside the classroom are the ones who may often have problems of their own outside the classroom.

Poor Conduct Disorder (PCD), sometimes referred to as Naughty Child Syndrome (NCS), or in the US as Oppositional Defiant Disorder, is where the child's persistent and prolific disruptive behaviour is not attributable to other neurological, psychological or emotional diagnoses. PCD is therefore more about nurture than nature; it occurs as a result of the child's conditioning rather than any genetic traits, injury or illness. This could be as a consequence of over-indulgent parents, resulting in the child always getting what they want and therefore always expecting to get what they want, or neglectful parents not taking an interest in their children, resulting in the child constantly seeking attention.

PCD is a condition which ranges from mild (where the child's conduct causes irritation) to moderate (where the child's conduct causes minor harm to others) to severe (where the child's conduct causes major harm to others).

Typical challenges facing children and young people who are suffering from NCS may include:

- experiencing difficulty forming relationships with their peers
- needing to talk out of turn or constantly move around the classroom
- frequently refusing to obey parents or other authority figures
- lacking empathy for others
- getting involved in arguments or fights
- having trouble following instructions
- lacking the ability to complete tasks without close supervision
- being disruptive when working in group tasks.

Early intervention and treatment of PCD is essential as the child with PCD may continue to be disruptive and anti-social into their teen and adult years, leading to violent behaviour, drug or alcohol abuse or criminal acts. This may have a significant impact on their relationships, career prospects and the general quality of life of the child, their family and their peers.

Strategies for dealing with *pop artists* include the following:

- Don't be afraid to invade their space. Walk over to them and conduct part of the lesson standing next to them.
- Direct firm, but not derogatory, comments at them. Ask them to be quiet. Let them know they are being unfair to their peers.
- Change approaches. If their disruptive behaviour is becoming more troublesome, change what you are doing. For example, break the class up into smaller groups for some activities.
- Avoid focusing on the negative: some *pop artists* are given numerous 'stop' directives and commands throughout the day, for example 'stop talking', 'stop fooling around', 'stop texting'. Although these statements get the point across, they may come across as negative and harsh in tone. In contrast, 'start' statements are short, positive reminders of the expectations and serve as a clear directive about what students should be doing.

- Exclude them if necessary. If your best efforts aren't working, ask them to leave the classroom for that class period.
- Seek help. If you are having to regularly exclude the *pop artist*, talk with colleagues. Ask them how they would handle the situation.
- Tell them how you feel. Inform them, outside of class, that their disruptive behaviour isn't acceptable and that you will impose sanctions if it continues.

It's very rare that *pop artists*, unlike some of the other challenging individuals you will have to deal with, enter your lesson with a well-thought-out plan to disrupt it, and it's often the case that the *pop artist* isn't aware of the disruption they are causing. A lot of the blame can be attached to social pressures they may be experiencing.

Ever thought that you had characteristics of the *pop artist*? That you had persistent and prolific annoying behavioural traits that cause children to switch off during lessons?

Example 3.12: Supply teacher collars pupil

The supply teacher at Alfie's school, a special educational needs school, was an ex-head with years of teaching experience. She was a baby-boomer who dressed smartly, but in the fashion of the '70s (a high starched collar being her trademark). When Alfie refused to participate in her lessons, his teaching assistant asked him what the matter was. Alfie told her, 'It's that collar she's wearing; it's doing my head in'.

THE PLAGIARIST

The *plagiarist* is the learner who lives off the knowledge and skills of their peers and falsely claims credit for others' ideas. They may often do this to mask their own inadequacies or promote their own position.

Example 3.13: Using a helping hand

Richard knew that one of his students, Marek, hadn't written the assignment. He just couldn't prove it. The depth of analysis and presentation of his work was way beyond

(Continued)

(Continued)

anything else he had produced before. This was an important assignment for Marek as 30% of his final marks rested on his score for this piece of work.

Not wanting to allow Marek to get away with it, Richard scrutinised the assignments of Marek's classmates. He found large chunks of Marek's work had been lifted almost word for word from another pupil's assignment. This prompted an internal investigation, during which Toni, Marek's classmate, admitted that she had tried to help him by letting him see what she had written. She claimed that she never thought Marek would just cut and paste her work. The results of the internal investigation deemed that Marek was to be awarded a score of 0% and Toni's score of 65% was downgraded to a minimum pass of 40%.

The plagiarist is arguably one of the more difficult of the challenging individuals to deal with. This is simply because you may not be able to prove conclusively that they are falsely claiming credit for someone else's ideas. Of course, if they blatantly claim credit for ideas that are clearly copied from other students or published works, you have proof of plagiarism and your organisation will have a policy for dealing with that. It may be more difficult when they have cut and pasted work downloaded from the internet. There is quite sophisticated software available for detecting this but it's worth weighing up the benefits of encouraging students to conduct research using the internet with occasional cutting and pasting. If they do this, however, tell them, 'for goodness sake, reference it!'

Although Marek's actions, and the way the issue was dealt with, took place outside of the classroom, there may be repercussions for the class in terms of the impact that this may have had on class morale and the possible friction between Marek (and maybe his friends) and Toni (and maybe her friends).

Two steps for dealing with *plagiarists* are as follows:

- Discourage plagiarism: explain that there is no problem with students using other people's ideas providing they acknowledge the source of their reference.
- Make sure that you have a policy for dealing with cheating. This will have to be in line with any policy that the awarding body has on cheating and must be applied consistently for all transgressions.

Some academics will claim that it is their right to use their learners' work in any papers that they write. This is nonsense! Refusing to acknowledge the source of any ideas is cheating, regardless of who the cheat is and who the source is.

THE DEFLECTOR

The *deflector* is the learner who fails to accept responsibility for their own actions and tries to blame others when things go wrong.

Example 3.14: It is not me

Glyn teaches a group of exceptional learners who work well together in class. One of the learners however, Nigel, regularly causes problems when the class is working on a group project. His biggest fault is consistently missing deadlines. When challenged over this, he points the finger at one of his classmates and claims it was their fault.

As part of an assessment, Nigel was working in a group that was making a model of the universe for a science project. He had responsibility for researching Venus and making a mock-up of the planet. When it came time for the group to present its model, he hadn't completed his task, blaming the others for not telling him about the presentation. Nigel's behaviour had a negative impact on the class. His classmates refused to work with him on future projects, claiming that they resented his attitude and his unwillingness to change his behaviour.

Learners who fail to accept responsibility for their actions do so for reasons that range from lacking interest in the task or the well-being of their team, to having a fear of failure or feeling overwhelmed by the scale of the task or expectations of their performance. Whatever the reason, if they continue to refuse to accept responsibility for their actions, they'll not only fail in their school work but also in their careers and relationships.

When this happens, teachers may sometimes react by either hoping the *deflector* will start to accept that blaming others isn't the best approach or not allowing them to work with others. Neither of these approaches is ideal. Hoping the problem will go away may have a detrimental effect on the group's performance on team tasks and excluding the deflector from team tasks will impact on their grades. Instead of this, teachers should aim to provide the *deflector* with the aptitude and attitude they need to be an effective team worker.

John Whitmore's (1998) GROW model is a simple but powerful way of helping people to accept responsibility for their actions. He likens the model to thinking about planning a journey in which you decide where you are going (the **Goal**), establish where you are at present (the **Reality**), explore the various routes (the **Options**) and are committed to reaching your destination (the **Will** to succeed). The model is an organic one that can be represented as in Figure 3.1.

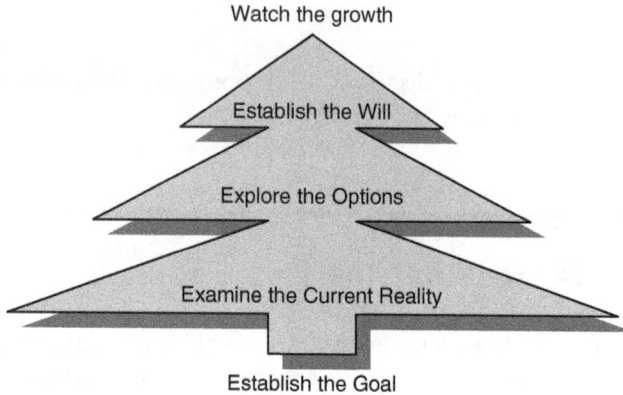

Watch the growth

Establish the Will

Explore the Options

Examine the Current Reality

Establish the Goal

Figure 3.1 The Whitmore GROW model

Source: Adapted from Whitmore, J. (2017) *Coaching Performance* 5e

The various constituents of the model can be summarised as follows:

- Establish the **Goal**: look at the behaviour that the other person wants to change and express this in terms of a Goal that they want to achieve.
- Examine the current **Reality**: encourage the individual to avoid trying to solve problems with their behaviour before considering where they are at present.
- Explore the **Options**: after exploring the reality, turn the person's attention to determining what is possible.
- Establish the **Will**: now that the options are clear, get the individual to commit to specific actions in order to move forward towards achieving their goal.

Whitmore stresses the importance of the teacher not considering themself to be an expert in the other person's predicament and not trying to solve their problems for them. He describes their ultimate role as being a facilitator who helps the person to select the best options.

The GROW model is possibly the most widely used of all of the behaviour modification models. It is relatively straightforward and the metaphor of organic growth is a good way of thinking about the model. The essence of good teaching, using this model, is asking good questions. Here are some useful tips and questions that you could ask the *deflector* at each stage:

- Talk to the *deflector*. Find out if there are circumstances that are contributing to their refusal to accept responsibility for their actions and whether they want to change their behaviour in this respect.
- Get them to set goals for changing their behaviour that are specific, measurable, achievable, realistic and time-bound. Ask them: 'When will they know that they have achieved their goal?', 'How confident are they that they can achieve the goal?' and 'What is a realistic schedule for achieving the objective?'

- Don't allow them to start coming up with solutions before they've even considered where they stand at present. Ask: 'What effect is their behaviour having on other people?', 'How do they feel about what is happening?', 'What have they been doing to date to address the issue?' and 'How does this issue impact on other issues they are facing?'
- Avoid coming up with the options. Remember that these are your options as to how you would tackle the situation. You should however get the individual to consider the viability of each of their options by asking: 'What are the possible repercussions of adopting this option?', 'What could they do if something goes wrong?' and 'What factors do they need to consider when weighing up an option?'
- Having explored the options, you now need to get the individual to commit to specific courses of action by asking 'What they will do next?', 'When will they do it by?' and 'How will they know that it's been done?'

Notice that all of the questions asked are open questions. Try to avoid asking closed questions that just require a 'yes' or 'no' answer. Make sure that when the person you are coaching responds to your question, you listen in an attentive and non-judgemental manner. In this respect, your body language may be more important than what you actually say.

Teachers can also be guilty of deflecting. Example 3.15 is the story of one of us in the 1960s, when studying for the Certificate in Secondary Education (CSE) in Geography.

Example 3.15: Nothing to do with me

Our geography teacher (and the school's deputy head) devoted several sessions to the subject of 'The Population in Australia', meaning people. Imagine our surprise when a large section of questions in the exam were on the 'sheep' population in Australia. The teacher blamed the examining board for the inadequacy of its briefing on the subject (and for most of us getting a low grade) when it was clear that he just hadn't read the brief carefully enough.

We may not have been any happier with the teacher if he had just admitted that he had made a mistake. Maybe as deputy head he felt that he needed to appear infallible by deflecting the blame elsewhere. A low grade in geography may not have had a massive impact on our careers but the lesson that it was OK for even the high and mighty to put the blame onto others probably did.

THE NARCISSIST

The *narcissist* is a learner who is totally self-absorbed. Their self-happiness is their own concern.

Example 3.16: I'm the one (for me)

Mandy was only 3 years old when her mother died of cancer. At the age of 13, she was described as *thirteen-going-on-thirty* and had assumed the role of housewife to her father. People were impressed by Mandy's devotion to her dad.

Things changed when Mandy reached the age of 16 and left school. She started a media studies course at college. Her boyfriend, Tim, was obsessed with her and gave her a series of expensive gifts. The more he gave her, the more Mandy seemed to demand. She appeared to be making good progress at college and had a series of glowing written reports. One day her father received a phone call from the college asking why Mandy had missed a tutorial. When her father looked into it, the glowing reports had all been forged and in fact Mandy was one step away from being excluded from the course. The college explained that it was only her devotion to caring for her disabled dad (another fabricated story) that convinced them to let her stay on the course. When her father challenged Mandy, she threw a tantrum and accused him of ingratitude for the sacrifices she had made for him and complained that the college was always picking on her.

Finding reasons to condone Mandy's narcissistic behaviour isn't easy. She could have been exhibiting poor conduct disorder (PCD) or suffering from post-traumatic stress disorder (PTSD) as a result of her mother's death. Some understanding of these conditions is therefore necessary.

Although PTSD is a psychological disorder normally associated with service veterans, it can develop in children or young people after they have lived through a particularly traumatic event, such as that experienced by Mandy. It can affect as many as one in seven children and young people and is more prevalent in girls than boys.

PTSD manifests itself differently in children or young people than in adults as they may have difficulty describing their feelings and discussing what caused it. There may be symptoms such as:

- *flashbacks*: this is where an individual involuntarily and vividly re-lives the event in the form of an action replay, a nightmare or repetitive and distressing images of the event
- *avoidance*: this is where an individual avoids people or places that remind them of the event
- *emotional numbing*: this is where an individual switches off from things and becomes isolated or withdrawn
- *hyperarousal*: this is where an individual becomes anxious about even minor things and has difficulty relaxing.

In most cases, PTSD develops within the first few days or weeks after a traumatic event. There may be cases however when the PTSD develops months or years after the event. Teachers of children or young people with PTSD can have a major impact on the success of treatment for this disorder. Younger children, particularly those who cannot explain their emotions, should be watched carefully for any signs of behavioural change that might signal the onset of PTSD. Early diagnosis and treatment of PTSD in children or young people are vital to ensure the individual lives a meaningful and productive life.

By now, we suspect that you are a bit fed up with trying to identify how much of a *shell* or a *bully* you are. Narcissistic teachers are the worst of the lot. They have little interest in anything other than their own needs and ambitions. A tutor on a postgraduate programme told one of his students how fed up he was with having his own research disrupted by having to tutor his students. The student wanted to tell him that his fees were paying his wages but he decided discretion was the better part of valour. If you suspect that you have narcissistic tendencies, do something about it or consider pursuing an alternative career.

3.3 GETTING THE BEST OUT OF CHALLENGING INDIVIDUALS

The characters in this section are vastly different from those in the previous section in that their behaviour is not intended to be a threat to other learners, but rather their sense of high or low self-worth may prove challenging to you or may be having a negative effect on other learners.

The characters are:

a. The **superstar**: the most gifted and talented learner in the class.
b. The **doubter**: the learner who has a low sense of self-worth.
c. The **movie star**: the learner who has a constant craving to be the centre of attention.
d. The **hermit**: the learner who doesn't associate with their teacher or their classmates.
e. The **sponge**: the learner who constantly needs to be stimulated and disrupts sessions that they feel are not challenging enough.
f. The **procrastinator**: the learner who always comes up with excuses for not meeting assignment deadlines or being late for or failing to attend classes.
g. The **prima donna**: the learner who masks their own inadequacies by feigning or fabricating illnesses.
h. The **iceberg**: the learner who believes the whole world is against them.
i. The **sycophant**: the learner who attempts to gain advantage by flattering you or behaving in a servile manner.
j. The **results merchant**: the learner who lacks any drive for long-term development and is just obsessed with getting the best results in the class.

THE SUPERSTAR

The *superstar* is the learner who is exceptionally gifted or talented. They may deal with this in a modest manner or they may intentionally or unintentionally overawe others in their class by their performance. This may lead to others feeling inadequate or doubting their own abilities. We met Nicole during an Ofsted briefing session (example 3.17).

Example 3.17: False assumptions

Nicole talked passionately about the children in her Year 2 class, especially Maxie. Maxie was 7 years old. Nicole told us that she was a confident, entertaining individual who conversed with adults in a very mature manner. She was a prodigious reader who had learned an impressive array of snippets of conversational French from a phrase book at the age of 5. Nicole told us how Maxie was excited about her role as Annie in a forthcoming stage show of the same name and when she sang one of the songs from the show, how impressed she was by how clear and true her voice was.

Nicole admitted that she was worried that Maxie was having difficulty making friends at school. When she discussed this with Maxie's parents, they told her that Maxie was finding school work far too easy and boring and was becoming more and more reluctant to go to school.

Nicole couldn't understand why she felt uneasy about Maxie. We suspect that she had an assumption about how children of Maxie's age should act, and the mismatch between her age and the way she conversed with her made her feel uncomfortable. Nicole knew that Maxie's parents were not pushy and neither were they what could be considered as exceptionally gifted or talented. Maxie's achievements were all down to her own self-belief and motivation. She was both a gifted and talented learner, but Nicole, like many others, felt uncomfortable in her presence.

The terms gifted or talented are often used to describe children, such as Maxie, who are achieving, or who have the potential to achieve, a level significantly in excess of their peers. In this respect, we can categorise such children into: gifted, if their ability is in one or more academic subjects; or talented, if their ability is more practical, for example in sport, music, art or the performing arts.

Having a learner with exceptional gifts or talents in your class will have an impact on the educational and social environment in the classroom. As a teacher, you will face challenges in your own attitude or reactions to them. Rather than feel intimidated by their gifts or talents, try to understand their learning patterns in order to be able to recognise the qualitative differences in their responses and levels of conceptualisation so that you can support their development.

There are positive and negative aspects of having *superstars* in the class. The positive side of this is that they may stimulate discourse in the class by:

- being intellectually curious
- having advanced reasoning ability, especially when dealing with abstract concepts
- displaying exceptional speed of thought, especially when responding to new ideas
- possessing good memory retention
- having acute powers of observation
- displaying a tendency to find creative solutions to problems.

The negative side of this is that they disrupt lessons by:

- being unwilling to follow instructions, preferring to do things their own way
- being withdrawn and reluctant to take part in group tasks
- manipulating people and their environment to make themselves feel better
- having a superior attitude to those around them
- finding inadequacies in others, things or systems to excuse their own behaviour
- being impatient, both with themselves and others.

Although it is widely accepted that learning will come easier to gifted and talented children, as their ability frequently outstrips their social and emotional development, they may find it difficult to relate to their peers and to conform. This may lead them to be confused about their development and about why they are behaving as they are.

Susan Leyden, an educational psychologist, suggests (2013) that developing strategies and approaches to dealing with gifted and talented underachievers should be an integral part of school policy. She argues that this needs to take account of the indicators and causes of underachievement and the methods that are appropriate for dealing with this.

Strategies for supporting *superstars* include the following:

- Accept them for who they are. Be aware of their gifts or talents but also their faults and idiosyncrasies.
- Show them respect. Make them aware that you respect them for who they are and not for how they look or what they can do.
- Make them aware that it is all right if they make mistakes and fail, providing they learn from this.
- Create an environment where they can be themselves. Encourage them to feel comfortable in asking challenging questions without fear of being mocked or ridiculed by their peers for being a show-off.
- Encourage them to try new things. Always praise effort as well as achievement in anything they do that may be out of their comfort zone.

- Challenge them. Make sure that tasks presented to them will challenge their thinking and encourage them to produce work that extends their existing knowledge and skills.
- Don't group them on tasks according to their ability. Have different levels of challenge within a task according to each individual's ability.
- Keep a lookout for any signs of resentment towards them coming from their peers.
- Ensure that they are meaningfully occupied throughout the lesson.

Let's look at probably the best film about school life ever made to understand more about the problem with teachers who think they are *superstars*.

KES

Kes is a 1969 film directed by Ken Loach. It is based on the 1968 book *A Kestrel for a Knave* by Barry Hines. It tells the story of a 15-year-old boy, Billy (played by David Bradley), who suffers abuse both at home and at school. At his home, in a working-class area of a Yorkshire town, Billy's elder brother regularly bullies him and his family neglects him. At school, he is ridiculed by most of his teachers, especially his sadistic PE teacher, Mr Sugden (wonderfully played by Brian Glover), and classmates because of his tendency to daydream.

Billy appears to be headed for a menial job with no future. Consequently, he has no motivation and little to look forward to, until one day he finds a stranded baby kestrel. Associating his own situation with that of the bird, he finds meaning in caring for it. He raises, nurtures and trains the kestrel, which he calls Kes. Kes's growth and development give Billy hope that one day he will also develop and gain the skills to fly.

Sorry, if you want to know what happens to Billy and Kes you will have to watch the movie or read the book. The whole point of including this as an example is the one scene in the film where Mr Sugden is taking a group for a football lesson. Billy hates football and has a habit of forgetting his football kit. He is made to wear an ill-fitting pair of shorts and told to play as goalkeeper. Sugden grabs the ball and tells everyone he is going to play centre forward. With all the good players on his team, Sugden scores the winning goal past a hapless Billy and subsequently runs a lap of honour, mobbed by his 'adoring team mates'.

Sugden's behaviour is typical of teachers who have an over-exaggerated sense of their own ability. This doesn't just apply to their performance on the sports field but can be apparent in the classroom as they employ jargon or rhetoric that is way beyond the comprehension of their learners and use this to inflate their own position as an expert in the subject.

THE DOUBTER

The *doubter* is the learner who has a low sense of self-worth. This can vary from believing that they are not as good as their classmates to a deep-rooted sense of paranoia which may be characterised by high levels of mistrust, suspicion and a belief that they are being treated unfairly.

Example 3.18: Find the spark and light it

Tom was 15 and throughout his school life had been racked with self-doubt. He was no less capable than any of his classmates; it's just that he seemed reluctant to accept this. Feeling that he would never reach the standard his teachers expected of him, he put less and less effort into his schoolwork. The more that this happened, the more the teachers became critical of him, calling him a 'waster'. The more they did this, the less effort Tom made. In effect, Tom was in a downward spiral.

One day, out of the blue, Tom produced an essay that his teacher considered remarkable. Tom's one passion in life was sport and he had been watching the Winter Olympics and the final performance of the Russian world pairs skating champions. He was so engrossed by their performance that he wrote about it and the emotions it had stirred in him. At first, his teacher doubted that Tom had written the essay but after talking to him realised that he was the author.

Much to his embarrassment, Tom was asked to read his essay out to the rest of the class. When he was reluctant to do this, his teacher read it to everyone. The stunned silence of the class was replaced with a few nods of approval. Although Tom couldn't look up, there was a smile on his face that betrayed his recognition that maybe he was capable of something good.

The self-fulfilling prophecy was a term introduced by Robert Merton (1948). It was based on Aristotle's belief that, if you have high expectations of a learner and they are aware of this, they will perform at a level that matches these expectations. Conversely, if you have low expectations of a learner and they are aware of this, their performance will suffer. Let's go to the pictures and a cinema classic to make sense of this.

Never underestimate the effect that you have on others. You, like the Wizard in the story in the next example, exert enormous power over your learners' lives and, through your attitude towards them, can turn them into successes or failures. Tell them they are doomed to fail and they may begin to accept failure as an inevitable consequence. Tell them they have the potential for greatness and watch them grow.

THE WIZARD OF OZ

How can you turn a coward into a hero, a dullard into a genius or an emotional vacuum into a great lover? That's exactly the challenge facing the Wizard in Frank Baum's immortal story of *The Wizard of Oz*. He gave the *Cowardly Lion* a medal for courage, the *Scatterbrain Scarecrow* a diploma and the *Tin Man* a ticking clock (well, Christian Barnard hadn't perfected his technique for heart transplants at this stage). You need to watch the movie to see what happens next.

Strategies for dealing with *doubters* include the following:

- Give them a few tasks that are relatively easy to complete. Acknowledge their achievement of the task. A simple 'well done' or nod of approval will do, but celebrating the achievement with others will have a great impact on their self-belief.
- Reward effort as well as achievement. Make sure that learners see the connection between effort and success.
- Get the learners in your class to share what they have learned with others. Develop a rapport within the class whereby learners acknowledge the efforts and successes of others. Simple nods of appreciation or a round of applause may be appropriate.
- Support them to learn from mistakes as well as successes. Teach the learners in your class how to handle the failures that inevitably they will experience from time to time.
- Make your learners aware that you have high expectations of them. Don't be unrealistic, however, as this may lead them to question whether they can meet your expectations.
- Encourage them to stop comparing their accomplishments to what their class-mates are achieving. Tell them that it's not their classmates who are setting the benchmark for achievements but they themselves.
- Tell them to stop worrying about what others are thinking about them. Convince them that worrying about what everyone else is thinking about them will inhibit them and hold them back from achieving great things.

It's not only the Toms of this world that doubt their ability. Oscar-winning star and one of the most acclaimed actors of her generation, Meryl Streep, confessed to having varying degrees of low self-confidence and self-loathing. She said, 'You can have a perfectly horrible day where you doubt your talent ... Or that you're boring and they're going to find out that you don't know what you're doing' (www.azquotes.com/author/14233-Meryl_Streep).

Just as you need to use positive language with students who doubt their ability, so it is important to employ positive self-talk. How many times have you told yourself that 'you can't do something', only to find out that you had talked yourself into defeat? Deal with this by creating a vision of the person you want to be. You will face a lot of negativity in your life. This will come from a number of angles, including your bosses, your peers and even your learners. Don't allow negative self-talk to undermine your ability.

Example 3.19: Recognise failings but celebrate strengths

When Annie left school, she found work in local factories. She married, had three children and returned to work serving dinners to children in a nursery. This led to playground supervision and then to one-to-one support for two girls with special needs. She followed one of the girls as she progressed into primary school as her statemented helper. Annie's enthusiasm for her work with children with additional learning needs (she always called them 'special children with needs') resulted in her being offered a teaching assistant (TA)'s post in the school. She worked there for a further 15 years until her retirement last year.

Annie's ability to work with children with the most challenging of needs and to do the messy tasks that most teachers refuse to do was never questioned and she was a trusted and respected member of staff at the school. Where Annie had problems was with her spelling, especially with homonyms. She told us that if she had a 50-50 choice with words like *there* and *their* or *where* and *wear*, she would make the wrong decision 80% of the time.

Annie is one of the few TAs who dreaded the summer holidays because it often meant having to return to work with new teachers or pupils and the fear that her spelling shortcomings would be exposed by them.

Annie was a victim of the *imposter syndrome*. This is something that plagues many NQTs, but it is not unheard of in educators of any level. The main symptoms are feelings of inferiority and fears that some day their inadequacies will be discovered. Annie failed to accept that the imposter syndrome is exactly that; it is a syndrome. It may feel real to her, but it's not. It's a completely irrational reaction to her negative thoughts.

Like all sufferers of the imposter syndrome, Annie needed to remind herself that she was hired to work in the school because she was deemed qualified to do so. Instead, she kept planting the seeds of self-doubt: 'What if I have to write a report on someone and I spell some words wrong?' With a lot of hard work, a handy dictionary and a book with some of the more common words that she was expected to use,

Annie slowly but surely lessened the effect of the imposter syndrome. 'It's still there', she told us, 'but not as bad as it used to be'. She finds that the spell check facility on her laptop is a godsend but not brilliant at dealing with some homonyms.

THE MOVIE STAR

The *movie star* is the egotistical learner who has a constant craving to be the centre of attention and an overwhelming need for admiration. They can vary from those who thrive on being the centre of attention to those who genuinely feel people are in awe of them.

Example 3.20: A unique tragedy

Throughout her school life, Kim hadn't progressed much above average in any of her subjects. Her school notes did indicate that following a sustained period of bullying, her parents had moved her to a different school. Kim was being bullied because of her quietness and lack of stature. Kim's survival strategy in her new school was to protect herself by taking on the demeanour of someone who was unique and special. She would go around shouting 'look at me, I'm so wonderful' and 'I've done this and that, I am so much smarter than you'.

Most of Kim's classmates tolerated her actions until unreasonable expectations of favourable treatment led her to try to take advantage of others in the class. One by one, she drove away people who had been close to her. She had exaggerated her abilities and talent, without commensurate achievements, to such a degree that she became a figure of scorn that far exceeded the ridicule she had experienced in her previous school. Unable to cope with this, Kim committed suicide: she was 14 at the time.

The *movie star* is different from the *superstar* in that their behaviour is characterised by a long-standing pattern of grandiosity (either in fantasy or actual behaviour) rather than exaggerated self-belief or arrogance. *Movie stars* often believe they are of primary importance in everybody's life or to anyone they meet, often with a complete lack of empathy for others. They sometimes display snobbish, disdainful or patronising attitudes. For example, an individual displaying this type of behaviour may complain about a classmate's 'rudeness' or 'stupidity' or make condescending remarks about their teacher. In an effort to gain superiority, they may try to inflate their own ego or try to deflate those of others.

There is a thin line between confidence, arrogance and egotistical behaviour. In the same way that for many years assertive women were looked on as aggressive (mostly by men who resented their talent), so confident people are often looked on as arrogant and arrogant people as egotists. The difference between arrogance and egomania is in the level of control over the behaviour. Arrogant people may only be arrogant in certain situations. For example, the footballer who beats three players before shooting past the goalkeeper and then nods as if this is something they can do for fun is looked on as arrogant. Egomaniacs, on the other hand, are the sort of players who try to claim credit for someone else's goal.

Strategies for dealing with *movie stars* include the following:

- Don't be afraid to bring them down to earth. Explain to them that if they are smart or talented, they don't need to go around telling people they are, as people will see it if it's there.
- Don't be too hasty to label someone as egotistical. There is a thin dividing line between confidence, arrogance and egotism. Make sure you know which of these states of mind the *movie star* is in.
- Don't let it get to you. Be charitable in interpreting this person's obvious exaggerations and assumptions about themselves and try to find ways to excuse some of their big talk.
- Change the topic of conversation. This can take the wind out of their sails and help to make it clear to them that you're not prepared to stand there all day to listen to their self-appreciation act.
- Refuse to be drawn in. Smile a lot, say very little and give an occasional nod of the head. Do this whilst you plan your exit.
- Politely question their claims. A simple technique is to use the 'Really?' comment. Say it initially with a mild tone of disbelief then increase the intensity as their claims become greater. Be careful when doing this that you don't overdo it and end up patronising them.
- Suddenly be incredibly busy. If they are determined to talk about themselves, keep them waiting for as long as you can get away with it. This technique often works very well because 'putting the *egomaniac* in their place' is the opposite of what they want.

Take a bit of time out to listen to what you are saying to your class. Are you always talking about yourself? Do you get mad or irritated if the centre of attention moves away from you to someone else? Are you frequently boasting about your achievements, dismissing others and behaving as if you know everything? Then I'm afraid you are showing signs of being a true *movie star*.

If you are prepared to take off those rose-tinted spectacles when you look at yourself in the mirror, then never be afraid to admit you are wrong or that your knowledge of a subject is outdated or that things you may have done are less fantastic than you have given yourself credit for. If you can do this, without sinking to the level of the *doubter*, there is hope for you yet.

THE HERMIT

The *hermit* is the learner who doesn't associate with their teacher or their classmates. They can vary from those who are extremely shy and reserved to those with more serious psychological conditions such as attachment disorder.

Example 3.21: Julie the hermit

Julie was four months old when she was adopted from a Siberian nursery. At 18 months, she was a healthy baby and was above average in terms of her talking and walking. Despite this, her mother was concerned that she didn't like being held, touched, being played with or read to. Her GP told her that he had encountered a number of adopted children, particularly from Eastern Europe, who had been traumatised or neglected and had difficulty attaching to their adoptive parents.

Julie's adopted parents were both professionals and in their 40s when they adopted Julie. Their fears in the GP's diagnosis were confirmed when Julie failed to interact with the other children in her nursery school. Staff strategies for dealing with this, which included acting passively when Julie was fussing and laughing at her when she threw a tantrum, confounded other parents. Although it took time, their approach worked and by the age of 6, Julie had become more attached to her parents and teachers.

Working with someone who has withdrawn from normal classroom activities can be frustrating and emotionally trying. It may be difficult working with a learner or young person who displays no capacity for connecting with you or responding to your efforts. It's important therefore that you and the learner's parents talk about what approach is best for the learner. An informed, cooperative and strong family–school team is vital to help the learner overcome the challenges they face with their behaviour and get the most out of their social and educational experiences.

Every learner or young person and their family are unique and there is no one set of emotions, thoughts or behaviours that typify every individual's desire for the need for isolation. There is however a substantial body of information available from organisations such as Mind to support teachers who work with children who have had specific experiences such as neglect or abandonment that resulted in an attachment disorder.

John Hattie (2012: 46) believed that how learners who are not engaging see themselves, and what they perceive as most important in terms of their learning and their desired outcomes, has a significant effect on their motivation to participate and their subsequent behaviour in class. He argued that research on the subject was divided into understanding the *structure* of self-concept (how we see ourselves) and the *processes* of self-concept (how we use what we find out about ourselves). He uses the metaphor of the *rope* to bring the strands together.

In the *rope model*, Hattie argues that there is no single strand underlying an individual's self-concept but many overlapping concepts of self. He categorises these as:

- **self-efficacy**: this is the confidence, or strength of belief, that learners have in themselves that they can achieve the desired outcomes
- **self-handicapping**: this occurs when learners allow self-imposed obstacles to get in the way of their achieving
- **self-motivation**: this can be intrinsic or extrinsic factors that drive the learner towards achieving the desired outcomes
- **self-goals**: these include mastery goals (something they can achieve through increased effort), performance goals (demonstrating expertise) and social goals (interacting with and relating to their peers)
- **self-dependence**: this occurs when learners become dependent on directions from their teacher and lack the capacity to regulate or evaluate their own performance
- **self-discounting and distortion**: this is when learners disregard positive and negative feedback from their teachers as not being worthwhile
- **self-perfectionism**: this is when learners set standards for themselves that may be too demanding and see it as a failure when these aren't met.

Hattie suggests that the strength in the rope lies not in any single strand but in the combination of many overlapping strands. He claims that, when any of the strands become weak, the learner will start to experience such a sense of helplessness that they feel they can't cope with the learning, the result being that they disengage with learning activities and turn to challenging behaviour as a protection measure against being looked on by their peers as the class failure.

Strategies for supporting *hermits* include the following:

- Encourage them to have the confidence or belief in themselves that they can achieve the desired outcomes.
- Convince them not to allow self-imposed obstacles to get in the way of their achieving.
- Don't allow them to become dependent on directions from their teacher and/or to lack the capacity to regulate or evaluate their own performance.
- Have realistic expectations of them.
- Accept that helping them is a long uphill journey and focus on small steps forward.
- Remain patient and celebrate small improvements as they occur.
- Be appreciative of their effort, not just their achievements.
- Remain positive. If they sense you are discouraged, they will become discouraged and may give up.

Because *hermits* are often mistrustful of others, creating an environment where they feel safe is a core issue. Building up their sense of security therefore should be at the forefront of what you do. You can achieve this by remaining calm when they are upset or not engaging in the lesson.

We're sure that your first reaction is to dismiss the thought that teachers can be *hermits*. We will admit that they are a rarity, but they do exist. One of us has a saying that goes something like 'never hide in front of the blackboard (or whiteboard)'. By this he means that teachers should never rely on writing lesson notes on the board or just reading from a textbook. This isn't teaching; it's just as Aristotle says: 'filling empty vessels rather than igniting flames'.

THE SPONGE

The *sponge* is the learner who constantly needs to be stimulated and disrupts sessions that they feel are not challenging enough. They vary from the over-enthusiastic learner with a thirst for knowledge to someone with an insatiable appetite for knowledge who, if this is left unfulfilled, will disrupt the class by constantly moaning about the inadequacies of your teaching and the stupidity of their classmates.

Example 3.22: A special case

Cassie was 14 and in her top set at school. She was described by her teacher, Les, as 'razor-sharp but a nightmare to work with because of her non-stop questioning'. It was inevitable that friction would start to grow between the two of them. On one occasion, Cassie was overheard by Les to describe his teaching as 'rubbish' and state that 'if she failed her exams it would be down to him'. Annoyed by this, Les began writing her a detention note. When Cassie saw this, she complained that he was being unfair to her and always picking on her.

Les had a bit of a dilemma here. He knew that he should be thriving on inquisitive learners but he felt that in the interests of the rest of the class, he just couldn't tolerate Cassie's behaviour any more.

Of course, the ideal is a class full of eager learners with a thirst for knowledge and participating enthusiastically in all classroom activities. If only this were true. Let's be clear here, we're not talking about this type of learner; the *sponge* will ask all of the questions, offer all of the answers and create a feeling amongst their classmates of 'why did I bother turning up?'. Are you getting the picture?

We suspect that *sponges* may be one of the most difficult of all of the challenging individuals to deal with. There is nothing offensive, abusive or passive about their behaviour. Their behaviour is, however, challenging in that, as in Cassie's case, it may make others abusive towards them and engender a feeling of passivity amongst the rest of the class with the approach of 'let's leave it to Cassie'.

Strategies for dealing with *sponges* include the following:

- Don't discourage them: never try to diminish their enthusiasm for the subject but do try to get them to harness it and give others a chance to participate.
- Make use of them: use them in group sessions to work with less knowledgeable or less enthusiastic members of the class.
- Have ground rules: make sure that you have a set of behavioural rules that both you and the individual sign up to. This should include them allowing others an opportunity to answer questions and you allowing them to answer a reasonable number of questions.
- Appreciate feelings: when setting rules know when frustration levels (including yours) are rising and when it may be appropriate to back off slightly.
- Be respectful: never ignore, ridicule or be openly critical of them or allow other members of the class to do so.

Sadly, there aren't enough *sponges* in the teaching profession. Taking up every opportunity to share your ideas with your learners, to learn from them and to build on each other's ideas is a critical aspect of good teaching and one that is often overlooked.

THE PROCRASTINATOR

The *procrastinator* is the learner who frequently fails to meet assignment deadlines and comes up with excuses for not meeting them.

Example 3.23: Punishment to fit the crime

Robert was 15 and hadn't done his English essay. Instead of doing his homework, he had attended a bonfire display. In desperation, and knowing he was going to be told off, he wrapped a bandage around his writing hand and said it had occurred at the bonfire and he had slight burns that prevented him from writing the essay. He may have gotten away with this had he not tried to embellish the story by saying that the incident involved a banger that had been thrown near a baby's pram and that as he tried to grab it, it went off in his hand.

(Continued)

(Continued)

Robert's teacher told him how impressed she was by his bravery and that she was going to recommend him for special mention in the school assembly. Robert went into modesty mode, saying that wasn't necessary. He went into panic mode when the teacher insisted. He went into relief mode when the teacher relented on the basis that he work through the pain barrier and write an essay about the 'boy who cried wolf'. At this stage, Robert realised he had been found out. Fifty years later, he still recalls that essay for which he was given a B+.

We guess that most teachers have a catalogue of excuses from their learners for not completing assignments on time. The likelihood is that they have probably used most of them themselves when they were learners. The tried and trusted 'dog ate my essay' has now been replaced by the 'printer chewing up the assignment'. The difficulty is proving that the excuses have been made up. You can't accuse someone of lying for not doing their homework. They may have a dog with a passion for consuming paper, or they may have performed a heroic act. Be careful, as you don't want to be facing a complaint over this.

The other side of the coin, however, is that you don't want to be duped or get a reputation for being a 'pushover'. The teacher in example 3.23 handled her learner brilliantly. She didn't accuse him of anything but did call his bluff and, when it turned out that he had spun a tale (and not a particularly good one at that), imposed a punishment that was entirely appropriate. Learn from this! If you want something more, here is an approach for managing time more effectively that you can teach your learners to use.

The approach is based on a quote from former American president Dwight Eisenhower who said: 'what is important is seldom urgent and what is urgent is seldom important'. The principle is generally represented as a 2 × 2 matrix (Covey, 2004).

The characteristics of each of the quadrants in the matrix are:

- *High Importance – High Urgency (HIHU)*: these are tasks that are critical and have to be done immediately.
- *High Importance – Low Urgency (HILU)*: these are tasks that are important but don't have to be done immediately.
- *Low Importance – High Urgency (LIHU)*: these are tasks that need to be done immediately but can be delegated.
- *Low Importance – Low Urgency (LILU)*: these are minor distractions and should be avoided.

By using the matrix to prioritise, you can deal with the urgent tasks, whilst, at the same time, working towards achieving your long-term goals. Do this as follows:

- Start by compiling a list of all the things you need to do (even the unimportant things). Write these on separate cards.
- Divide your desk into four quarters (representing the quadrants in the matrix). Place each card in the respective quarters denoting HIHU – HILU – LIHU – LILU (does this sound like an audition for a yodelling choir?).
- Take out those cards in the LILU quarter of the desk and shred them! Hang on, before doing that, just check to see if any of them have the potential to become LIHUs. If they do then don't shred them just yet.
- Now work on the HIHU quarter. Take each activity card in turn, put them in order of priority and take the necessary action to deal with the activity. With some activities, a little bit of action might relegate them to the HILU or LIHU piles. Don't stop until you have cleared all the activities in that quarter.
- This is where you make a choice of dealing with the HILU or LIHU activities. We suggest that if time is incredibly tight you go for LIHU first. If you have more time to play around with, go for HILU. Don't stop until you have cleared all the activities in those quarters.
- Now go back to the LILU quarter and deal with all the activities left, shredding the ones that are nothing more than distractions.

If you didn't find time to do this exercise properly then put it in the HIHU box as it will significantly improve your time management.

Strategies for dealing with *procrastinators* include the following:

- Never openly accuse them of lying to you about not doing an assignment on time. Even if you are certain they are not telling the truth, the long-term damage this can create is not worth making the accusation.
- Ask questions to ascertain the legitimacy of an excuse: don't make this like the Spanish Inquisition. You don't want to appear to be accusing them but you do need to find out if they are spinning you a tale.
- Talk to other teachers: it's worthwhile finding out if they aren't handing in work on time to other teachers. If not, it could be that they are having problems with your subject.
- Teach them time-management techniques: we believe that the one suggested above is the best but there are others on the website www.about.com/education.

We once heard a joke that the only person who ever gets his work done by Friday is Robinson Crusoe. Most teachers we talk to these days express their love of teaching but confess a dislike for the paperwork that accompanies this.

THE PRIMA DONNA

The *prima donna* is the learner who seeks sympathy from all around them. They vary from learners who do this just to crave attention to those who may be suffering from psychological conditions such as hypochondria or Munchausen's syndrome.

Example 3.24: Treating the cause

Jenny, a 12-year-old girl, had no history of ear infection, surgery or disease that affects the ears like meningitis. She reported to the school nurse that she was having daily discharges from her ear. The nurse referred Jenny to her GP who in turn made an appointment for her to see an ear, nose and throat specialist. She was admitted to hospital for four days for observation. During this time, there was no discharge from her ears. Once she returned to school, the discharges returned.

Jenny's father had been diagnosed as having schizophrenia and her mother was paraplegic. She had been living with an aunt since starting secondary school. Her aunt had provided three small tubes filled with samples of the discharge. Jenny was hospitalised again and after three days of being observed closely was seen to fabricate her illness by filling her ear canal with a mixture of water and spit. Despite evidence to the contrary, Jenny denied that she had been faking her illness. She was referred for psychiatric consultation and diagnosed as having Munchausen's syndrome.

Only a very small number of *prima donnas* actually have a psychological disorder. Most are merely attention seekers. Munchausen's syndrome is a personality disorder where an individual fabricates or fakes symptoms of illness in an attempt to mislead others about their situation. The condition was named after an 18th-century German dignitary, Baron von Munchausen, who made up stories about his life to gain attention.

In Jenny's case, the turmoil in her family life and the overwhelming desire for sympathy caused her to fabricate the ear condition. What was particularly distressing about Jenny's case was her refusal to accept that she had faked the illness. There was also a suspicion that her aunt had helped in the deceit. When a parent or caregiver who is closely associated with a learner causes or fabricates symptoms in the learner, in an attempt to mislead others about the learner's condition, it is known as Munchausen by Proxy Syndrome (MBPS). Someone might act in this way if they have a need for attention and sympathy from healthcare or educational professionals, to obtain state benefits for themselves or the learner, or to gain the satisfaction of deceiving others who they perceive to be more important or powerful than they are.

In the most severe cases of MBPS, challenging individuals may go to great lengths to make the learner sick by switching their medicines, infecting them, giving them sugar or salt intensified foods or placing blood or urine specimens in the learner's underwear. Although it is estimated that around 80% of perpetrators of MBPS are the learner's mother, not all of them are parents. There are instances of the learner's siblings or friends using MBPS to divert attention away from their behaviour and professionals using MBPS to gain resources for medical or educational programmes.

The long-term prognosis for children who are victims of MBPS depends on the degree of damage caused by the perpetrator and the time taken to diagnose it. Some children experience distressing symptoms such as mental retardation, brain damage or long-term physical impairments as a result of the perpetrator's actions. There is an estimated 7–8% increase in the mortality rate amongst MBPS victims, with one in four suffering psychological and emotional trauma for periods of two or more years after the abuse. Even when the perpetrator and learner are separated, the learner may come to believe that love and attention can only be gained when they are ill and develop Munchausen's syndrome themselves. There are some bizarre stories about children and young people suffering as a result of MBPS.

Example 3.25: Victims of fantasy

In 2008, Leslie Wilfred called her husband, Chris, to tell him that the twins she had been carrying for five months had been stillborn. The grief-stricken mother told her husband that the twins had been cremated and she wanted a full funeral for them. It was only after a very emotional and distressing period for the Wilfred family that the truth came out that the twins had not died; they had never existed. The entire pregnancy had been fabricated by Leslie Wilfred.

When the authorities looked into the case, they found an alarming series of incidents involving the family's other five children (four from a previous relationship by Leslie and one from Chris). This included allegations that Chris's son was prone to violent rages, that one of Leslie's sons needed a gallbladder removal as a result of persistent vomiting, that one daughter was allegedly dying from leukaemia and another was suffering from a psychological disorder as a result of being raped. It was only after an investigation by the learner protection services that none of the claims made about her children's conditions were substantiated; even the alleged rape had never been reported. A number of disturbing facts emerged from the investigation, including Chris's son being made to sleep in a small box every evening to 'protect' the family from his alleged 'threatening' behaviour.

After a two-year investigation, Leslie Wilfred was found guilty of several counts of cruelty and sentenced to eight years in prison. Remarkably, her husband Chris was considered to have been ignorant of all but one count of the acts of cruelty. The officer investigating the case believed that if they had not intervened when they did, there would have been fatalities within the family. The children involved had not suffered permanent physical damage but the emotional distress caused would have a long-lasting impact on their lives.

Strategies for supporting a learner or young person who you suspect is fabricating an illness or is a victim of MBPS include the following:

- Support them to develop a more realistic understanding of their health.
- Encourage them to learn the difference between the lies perpetrated about their health, and reality.
- Encourage them to talk to you about what's happening to them.
- Always consider their safety as your prime concern.
- Report any concerns you have to the school's appointed child protection officer.
- Look out for signs of self-harming.
- Take any accusations of MBPS seriously until you know for sure they are not true.
- Never openly confront the alleged perpetrator.
- Help the victim to recover after the abuse has stopped.
- Talk to them about any misguided sense of loyalty they have to the perpetrator, and any feelings of guilt they may have for reporting the perpetrator's actions.

Whilst not all suspicions of Munchausen's syndrome or MBPS turn out to be true, all deserve serious consideration and immediate action.

We saw a cartoon recently where Joe is refusing to get out of bed and go to school. 'I'm feeling ill', he tells his mum. 'The others all hate me. They keep calling me names'. 'But darling', his mother tells him, 'You must go in; you're their teacher'.

Faking illness, or genuinely feeling that you are ill, despite no clinical evidence to prove it, has become more prevalent as the pressures of teaching have increased. According to the Department of Education, the average number of days lost in the school year 2016–17 per teacher due to sickness was 7.4, with one in 83 teachers on long-term leave due to stress and mental health issues. This represents a 5% rise compared with the situation in 2015–16 and the indications are that this will increase even more as the pressures on the teaching profession continue.

THE ICEBERG

The *iceberg* is the 'oppositional angry' learner who believes the whole world is against them and who has built a defensive wall around themselves as a protection against the comments of teachers, parents and peers. For the most part, *icebergs* behave in a passive manner. This often turns to extreme introspection or acts of an aggressive nature when they are riled.

Example 3.26: Lighting a sensitive fuse

Connor was 12 when Vic started teaching him. There was something about Connor that disturbed Vic. It wasn't fear but that sense of dread that you get when you think something bad is going to happen. Vic wasn't alone in this respect; other teachers had similar feelings towards Connor. It wasn't that people particularly disliked Connor and nothing untoward had happened in the first term to give Vic reason to impose any sanctions on him.

Connor didn't have any close friends in the class and preferred to work on his own. On the occasions when he was asked to work with others, he became agitated and Vic noticed Connor constantly tapping his toes on the floor. When one of his classmates said that Connor had got something wrong, Connor left the room. He returned after a few minutes and when the same classmate made a derisive comment about his absence, Connor just flew at him, with a flurry of punches. Vic had to restrain Connor and remove him from the class.

After a brief period of suspension, Connor was allowed to resume his studies in Vic's class on the understanding that he attended anger-management classes. Connor is now 16 and a valued member of the school football team. His trial period with the local professional club ended because of concerns over his aggressive behaviour on the pitch. There were never any repeats of Connor's aggression in the classroom, however, and Vic noticed a significant improvement in his behaviour. The boy that he punched is now his best friend.

It's important to distinguish between the *iceberg* and the *bully*. The *iceberg* doesn't feel the need to physically or intellectually intimidate others. Their normally passive behaviour only turns to aggression when someone pulls the wrong trigger; it's what lies beneath the surface that needs to be dealt with (hence the analogy with an iceberg). In Connor's case, it was people poking fun at him and his reaction was to punch out. Other *icebergs* react differently and their reaction might be more verbal or consist of further withdrawals into isolation.

Strategies for dealing with *icebergs* include the following:

- Identify what the triggers are. It's important that the learner understands that the problem is their behaviour and not them. If the triggers are being pulled deliberately by others then it's their behaviour that needs to be dealt with.
- Explain that feeling angry is OK. Tell them that anger is like any other emotion, and there are times that it is appropriate to feel angry, but this must be with the right person, at the right moment, for the right reason.
- Be a good role model. If you lose your cool in class, they'll have trouble understanding what's appropriate and what isn't.
- Share with them what makes you angry. Create opportunities for you to talk about what makes you angry and how you deal with your feelings. Encourage them to open up about their feelings.

- Establish anger ground rules. Create classroom rules that make it clear what learners can do when they feel angry and what sorts of behaviour will result in a consequence.
- Encourage them to develop coping strategies. Teach them to take a break when they are becoming angry and how to relax by doing something enjoyable.
- Teach them conflict-resolution skills. These will help them learn how to resolve conflict peacefully and learn when to walk away when they are angry before they become aggressive.
- Let them know the consequences of being able to, and not being able to, control their anger. Children need positive consequences (an acceptable reward system) when they follow the anger rules and negative consequences (sanctions) when they break the rules. Find out what rewards they cherish and what punishments they fear.

There are a number of methods involving meditation and therapy outlined in Bates' book *A Quick Guide to Special Needs and Disabilities* (2017) for dealing with anger and other conditions. We'd like to highlight two which we feel are powerful tools for working with children with anger issues.

Cognitive behavioural therapy (CBT) was developed by Dr Aaron Beck in the 1960s (Beck and Beck, 2010). CBT focuses primarily on the thoughts and emotions (the causes) that lead to certain unwanted behaviours rather than attempting to eliminate the symptoms of unwanted behaviour. Over the past 50 years, there has been significant growth in the use of CBT, especially in dealing with anger. Although it was originally intended solely for adults, CBT practices have been widened over the past 20 years. CBT therapists now work with children to get them to reconsider their assumptions about themselves, to identify the thoughts and emotions that are causing their anger and to see that, by changing the way they view themselves and their environment, they can improve their condition. In order to be effective, however, CBT therapists need to encourage the child to open up about what's affecting their thoughts and emotions and to generate more positive thoughts about their situation and their ability to cope with it. This may prove challenging as many younger children, especially those with anger-related psychological disorders, may feel overwhelmed by their inability to control their anger and see improvement as impossible. CBT attempts to break down the improvement into bite-sizeable, manageable steps.

Mentalisation-based treatment (MBT) was developed by Anthony Bateman and Peter Fonagy in the 1990s (2006, 2016). It differs from the more traditional behavioural therapies in that it focuses primarily on the understanding that an individual has of their intentions and the intentions of others. It was originally designed for working with people with borderline personality disorder (BPD) but can also be used to work with anyone who is exhibiting behavioural problems or problems in sustaining any form of meaningful relationship.

The theories that underpin the process of mentalisation are as follows:

- Everyone has the ability to ascribe intentions and meaning to human behaviour.
- It is predicated on the belief that ideas shape interpersonal behaviour.

- It shapes our understanding of ourselves and others.
- It is central to human communications and relationships.

In MBT, the therapist focuses on the client's difficulty in recognising the effects that their behaviour has on other people and their inability to empathise with others. It is based on the concept that people with behaviour disorders have a poor capacity to take a step back from their thoughts about themselves and others and to mentalise or rationalise whether these thoughts are valid. In this respect, the therapist takes on a fairly active role by encouraging the individual to reflect on their current interpersonal interactions and relationships. This is described as a process of curious exploration and investigation.

Take responsibility for your behaviour when you lose your cool in front of your kids. Apologise and discuss what you should have done instead. Say, 'I am sorry that I shouted at you today when I was angry with you. I should have gone for a walk to cool off instead of raising my voice'.

THE SYCOPHANT

The *sycophant* is the learner who attempts to gain advantage by flattering you or behaving in a servile manner. They have a tendency to hang on to your every word, agreeing with every idea, thought or comment you make and volunteering to run errands or do odd jobs for you. They vary from those who have a genuine sense of admiration for your teaching but go overboard in letting you know about this, to those who strategically prey on your needs and weaknesses to build a favourable impression.

Example 3.27: Trying too hard to please

None of her teachers seemed to have a bad word to say about Andrea. She was a regular attendee in Jane's class – punctual, attentive, eager to please and always openly appreciative of Jane's teaching. In many respects, she was the model pupil. There were two incidents that made Jane question this.

First, during some down time in the staff common room, one of the members of staff asked Jane if it was true about one of her pupils glue sniffing. When Jane asked how the other teacher had heard about this, she said that Andrea had told her. Within a few minutes, two other members of staff commented that Andrea had also told them about the antics of other members of her class. When Jane confronted Andrea about

(Continued)

(Continued)

her allegations, she admitted that she had made them up because the others were getting more attention than her.

Second, like other classes in the school, Jane's class had a weekly Monday morning charity collection. Andrea was the volunteer who collected donations from the class. In the following morning's school assembly, the class which collected the most money was announced. Jane's class regularly won this accolade. Andrea's mum was concerned that Andrea was not eating properly and contacted the school. When Jane checked up on this, she discovered that Andrea had regularly skipped lunch. It appears that Andrea was using her lunch money to supplement the charity collection to make her collection efforts look good.

When Jane confronted Andrea about this, Andrea's response was that 'she couldn't eat her lunch thinking about all of those starving children in Africa'. When Jane gave the responsibility for the weekly collections to another member of the class, the amount of money collected dropped significantly as Andrea returned to eating lunch. Andrea also refused to talk to her replacement.

Example 3.27 indicates the two sides of the *sycophant*: the classroom gossip who tries to demean their peers to enhance their own position in the class and the willing volunteer who will undertake any tasks to curry favour. Both can have dangerous consequences. First, allegations of illegal or abusive activity of any description have to be investigated. This can be both time-consuming and, even if unfounded, can damage an individual's reputation and classroom or school morale. Second, allowing someone to do all of the jobs will create inter-class rivalry that could lead to friction or conflict in the class, especially if the *sycophant*'s classmates believe, rightly or wrongly, that you are favouring the *sycophant*.

You will find *sycophants* in every classroom. Every comment and compliment they make is designed to flatter you and make you look good. OK, so what's wrong with that? We all like a bit of admiration, even some uncritical approbation every now and then. Such blatant actions can however become nauseating both for you and the *sycophant*'s classmates, who can grow to despise them as the teacher's pet.

Assessing the legitimacy of any admiration or enthusiastic offers of help is easier said than done. It can be tempting to want to bask in the unabated glory of flattery. But remember that *sycophants* operate with a manipulative intent and build a favourable impression with you to further their personal goals, sometimes to the detriment of their classmates. If it's not dealt with effectively, it can encourage others in the class to resort to similar behaviour as a means of promoting their self-interest. This could even engender classroom rivalry as everyone attempts to outdo the others in flattering you. In this situation, no one in the class wants to question your teaching or point out your mistakes. As your ideas and information go unchallenged, it insulates you from criticism, which can result in ineffective teaching and, ultimately, poor learner performance.

Strategies for dealing with *sycophants* include the following:

- Be resistant: don't fall victim to their gossip or flattery or do anything that will allow them to take advantage of you.
- Don't overreact: appreciate that although complete agreement with what you say is often interpreted as a suspicious attempt to curry favour, it could also stem from honest appraisal of your teaching.
- Point out the consequences of their behaviour: make them aware of the impact that their actions have on others in making them appear toady or grovelling.
- Play them at their own game: test their motives by proposing ridiculous suggestions and seeing the reaction. If it still evokes eager nods, you may be facing someone with manipulative intent.
- Cross-check with others: try consulting other teachers. Is the learner behaving in the same obsequious manner with others? If so, how are those teachers handling the situation?
- Challenge them upfront: tell them that their flattery is neither expected nor tolerated.

Never admit to yourself that you don't have classroom favourites. If you do, you are only kidding yourself. You are, after all, only human and there will be some personalities that you favour above others. Heaping undeserved lavish praise on them and ignoring mistakes in their work however will do them no favours. They may come to expect this from others who are less sycophantic than you. Conversely, don't be over hard on them because you don't want to be accused of favouritism. Always try to be objective and consistent in the way that you deal with all learners.

THE RESULTS MERCHANT

The *results merchant* is the learner who lacks any drive for long-term development and is just obsessed with passing assignments.

Example 3.28: Peter the Great

Peter was considered a brilliant pupil by his teachers. He passed four A levels with outstanding grades and the Oxbridge entrance exams. He was the first pupil ever from his school to have achieved this. His potential was recognised early by the

(Continued)

(Continued)

school, but so was his disruptive behaviour. When he was in Year 13, he rigged a minor explosion in a chemistry class that destroyed equipment and came close to hurting someone. He had avoided being excluded from school due to the prestige his achievements gave the school.

Peter was an exceptional pupil but sacrificed a lot of his formative years in his attempt to get outstanding grades. Although he passed his entrance exams for Cambridge, he failed the interview. Disappointed at this, and thinking that anything less than Cambridge was a come-down, he decided to take a year out of education. He never returned to his studies.

Peter is now in his mid-30s. After spells of homelessness and a caution for shoplifting, he is now in a stable relationship and works in a charity shop. He appeared to be at a very content phase in his life. He told us that his life may have taken a different course if he had been excluded by the school for causing the explosion or if he had settled for a university other than Cambridge. People's expectations of him were too much for him to handle.

Peter was, in many respects, a high achiever in academic terms but low in terms of his personal development. His subsequent drop-out from education and society is evidence of this. What follows are two models that could have helped Peter.

Abraham Maslow's *hierarchy of needs* (1993) suggests that a person's motivation to do things is driven by what needs they have at a particular moment in time. The lower-order needs relate to the physiological and safety aspects of learning (physical and psychological). The higher-order needs involve belonging, self-esteem and self-actualisation. Maslow argued that progression to the higher levels is not possible unless lower-level needs have been met. Maslow's hierarchy of needs is represented in Figure 3.2.

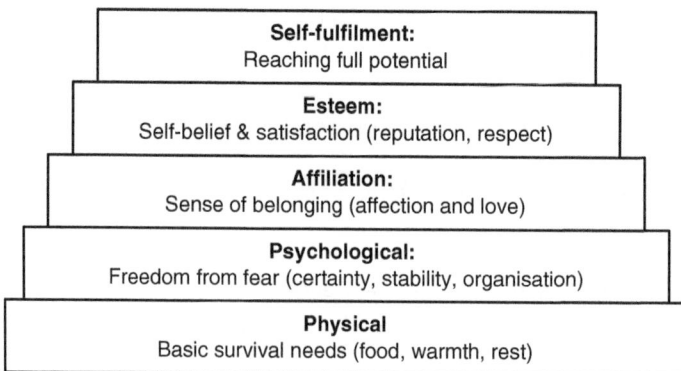

Self-fulfilment:
Reaching full potential

Esteem:
Self-belief & satisfaction (reputation, respect)

Affiliation:
Sense of belonging (affection and love)

Psychological:
Freedom from fear (certainty, stability, organisation)

Physical
Basic survival needs (food, warmth, rest)

Figure 3.2 Maslow's hierarchy of needs

Maslow suggested that an individual's reaction to something is dominated at any given moment by whichever one of the needs has priority. In Peter's case, his priorities were being determined by his teachers. They wanted a Cambridge graduate so much that they ignored Peter's personal development and school policy and procedure that would have dictated Peter was excluded.

Maslow argued that not everyone will experience self-actualisation in its full sense but many will enjoy periods of *peak experience* when they derive a sense of achievement at mastering a skill. Don't feel that it is down to you to ensure that everyone's needs are fully met. People can, and do, function in various states of contentedness. They also have expectations from you that, although conditions may not always be perfect, they should at the very minimum be tolerable. Peter's achievement gave him a sense of power over others, but it is clear that Peter's teachers drove him too hard.

Clayton Alderfer (1972) maintained that human motivation could be separated into three distinct categories: *existence* (survival or physiological well-being), *relatedness* (good interpersonal and social relationships) and *growth* (achievement of respect and self-actualisation). He argued that there was a progression from *existence* to *growth* through *relatedness* driven by satisfaction and a regression in the opposite direction driven by frustration. This can be represented as in Figure 3.3.

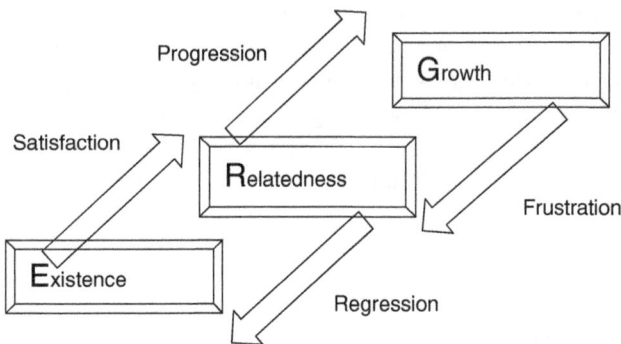

Figure 3.3   Alderfer's ERG model

Source: Adapted from Alderfer, C.P. (1969) 'An Empirical Test of a New Theory of Human Need'. *Psychology Review*

Alderfer claims that, although there is a progression from *existence* to *growth*, the likelihood of regression shouldn't be ignored and in some instances may be necessary to ensure learners are given every opportunity for personal growth.

The main difference between this model and Maslow's hierarchy of needs is that Alderfer stresses the importance of addressing all three needs simultaneously and accepts that regression to a lower level might not be a bad thing.

Here are some tips on how to deal with *results merchants*:

- Ensure that their basic needs are being met. These are issues that are sometimes taken for granted, such as their physical and psychological well-being.

- Encourage social interaction within the class. Make sure that in any small group activities, you mix the learners around so that they are given an opportunity to work with each other.
- Respect them. Learners will want to feel respected by you, so show them that you care for them by taking time out to find out about their interests.
- Celebrate success. Learners will want to feel a sense of pride in their achievements. Praise from you when they come up with new ideas and original solutions to problems is good but praise from their peers is even better, so get them to share their ideas with the rest of the group.
- Be realistic. Accept that you may only have a limited amount of control over whether or not your learners achieve self-actualisation.
- Acknowledge effort as well as achievement. This will go a long way to helping learners on their journey to self-actualisation.
- Accept regression. Remember that there may be points on the learning journey when your learner needs to turn back or regress to one of the lower levels. If this happens, work with them to ensure they don't regress beyond the point of no return. This will require some understanding on your part and acceptance that you may have to do something to support them.

In an age where there is a pre-occupation with SATs tests and exam results, most teachers will love the *results merchants*; they make them and their school look good. We guess that the question here is: what is the purpose of education? If the answer is just to improve the capacity of learners to gain good grades then long live the *results merchants* because they will make you look good. If we are looking for all-round individuals who can make a contribution to society then personal development should be more important.

SUMMARY OF PART 3

In Part 3, we've looked at a range of characters that you might find in the classroom. These vary from those who intimidate others through their aggressive and often abusive nature, through those with persistent or prolific annoying habits, to those who just refuse to participate in lessons.

Classroom dynamics is a fascinating area of study. Thankfully, you will never be faced with a homogenous mass of learners. Teaching would be a boring profession if everyone had the same abilities, the same learning style, the same characteristics, and presented the same challenges. The converse of this, however, are the challenges that you face with a group of individuals who display some of the more extreme characteristics of those listed in Part 3.

We suppose that you want to know how to handle a situation like this. Before we make some suggestions on this, look through the following scenarios, which range from primary through to post-compulsory vocational education, and think about how you would handle the situation. These are all real scenarios experienced by the contributors to this book. Although you may think it more expedient to just concentrate on your own particular teaching area, you may be able to learn something from all of the scenarios. Once you have done this, go to Appendix 4 for some ideas.

Scenario A: You are the acting head teacher (AHT) of a small, rural primary school. You have a 50% teaching timetable and this morning have just returned with a Year 5/6 class from a swimming lesson at the local baths. The lesson is timed such that the children will arrive back in school after morning break has finished. You supervise them for ten minutes on the playground before returning to class with them for their mathematics lesson. As usual, there are dawdlers but the last boy to arrive is upset, telling you that he found his towel stuffed down a toilet. What do you do?

Scenario B: You have spent some time during the lunch break preparing for the first lesson in the afternoon. Your plans and expectations are disrupted as learners arrive in a state of excitement (unfortunately not of anticipation). During the break, there has been a disagreement between two members of the class. Both are unwilling to terminate their dispute and are being egged on by several members of the class who are vocal in their support for one or other of the protagonists. What do you do?

Scenario C: Midway through a lesson that is being well received by the great majority of learners, a learner makes a racist remark. Though not having previously expressed themselves in such an unpleasant manner, you have a number of reasons to believe this learner and his family have entrenched racist views and object to the school values which you fully support and articulate in your teaching. You suspect the learner's reaction is deliberately provocative and confrontational and an open challenge to school policy. What do you do?

Scenario D: Twenty minutes after the start of the day's first lesson, the deputy head teacher brings a late arrival into your class. They are just as unwilling to enter your classroom as they were to enter the school building ten minutes earlier. On entry, they are vocal in their protestations which continue after the departure of the deputy head. Their behaviour continues to be vocal and uncooperative and it is disrupting what, up until their arrival, had been a promising lesson. You suspect the catalyst for this behaviour is something that has occurred at the learner's home which may need sensitive discussion, but feel pressured as you are at a critical point in the lesson. What do you do?

Scenario E: The school is under pressure to improve its results which is impacting directly on you because you teach a group of pupils whose grades in the end-of-year tests are crucial if the school is to be seen to be raising standards. You have therefore meticulously planned your teaching to expose pupils to a programme focused on developing skills and understanding in key subjects, including organising a number of interventions within and outside of school hours to support pupils. Whilst this appears to be having a positive impact on the majority of pupils, you are aware that a minority have become less motivated by changes that are intended to support them. The behaviour of one or two pupils has also deterio-rated, despite them receiving small group and individual tuition. What do you do?

Scenario F: Charlie is a demotivated learner who, despite your best efforts, avoids work and indulges in uncooperative behaviour. He is a strong character and influ-ential with other class members. You feel that this is having a detrimental effect on attitudes to learning and behaviour and are fearful that it will deteriorate further. What do you do?

Scenario G: You follow the school's positive behaviour policy which seeks to identify and reward good behaviour and have been actively implementing it with a small group of learners who are potentially disruptive. This has reduced instances of bad behaviour by the group as they amass rewards. You are aware that there are learners whose good behaviour is less frequently acknowledged because it is the norm. Your unease at the possible inequality of your actions appears to be confirmed by one of the better motivated members of the class who draws your attention to it. What do you do?

Scenario H: You have a Year 8 food technology lesson. You start the lesson with the usual health and safety instructions regarding the tools, utensils, materi-als, equipment, etc. to be used – in other words, the 'do's and don'ts'. After the introductory element, students turn to the practical element and the session is progressing well when you notice a knife is missing from the knife block – it was in place at the start of the lesson and, in view of the activities, there is no reason for a knife to have been removed from the block. What do you do?

Scenario I: You work in a co-educational independent public school for 11–18-year-old students. The school has boarders as well as day students. You are in your first term of teaching. After school, whilst you are supervising boarding students who are preparing for tea or doing homework or engaging in a leisure activity, a Year 10 girl tells you that she saw another girl in her form using a mobile phone to take photographs of girls in the changing room after a PE lesson – it was the last lesson of the day. Some of the girls in the changing room would have been day students, others would be boarders – the alleged photographer was a day student and had by now left the school for the day. In disclosing what had hap-pened, the girl named her classmate and added that the girls did not know they were being photographed. She hadn't told anyone. Students were allowed to have mobile phones in school but they were to be switched off in lessons and placed where they could be seen at all times by a member of staff. Boarders also had out-of-school access to their phones but there were certain restrictions regarding usage. All parents had signed forms allowing or not allowing their children to be photographed – the forms listed occasions when they could be caught on camera (for example, in team photographs, magazine articles, visits). What do you do?

Scenario J: You are teaching on an Access to the Police Force course. The learners are aged between 17 and 21. The group is mixed in terms of social and educa-tional backgrounds. There is a problem developing in class between two of the learners. Nigel is a young graduate with little experience of life. He appears over-confident and patronising to the less well-educated members of the group. Dave is one of the more mature learners with some experience of working on a building site. He is a know-all, aggressive and argumentative individual who is prejudiced against anyone who has had a good education. He directs his aggression at Nigel and, to a lesser extent, at you. The situation is beginning to get out of hand. What do you do?

Scenario K: You are teaching on a horticulture course. The learners are aged between 19 and 24. Ellen is one of the more mature learners with some experience of working in horticulture. You sense that other learners are becoming increasingly irritated by her continual boasting. It is obvious that she is undermining the self-confidence of the group. What do you do?

Scenario L: You are teaching on a day release course in building trades. The learners are aged 17–19 years. On the whole, they are a conscientious group who apply themselves to set tasks. A couple of the group have set themselves up as class *jokers* and are constantly joking and talking throughout your demonstrations. You have tried to stop this by asking them to be quiet, but they take no notice. What do you do?

Scenario M: You are teaching 16–17-year-olds on a basic skills course which is taught in tandem with a beauty therapy course. There are three learners who persistently disrupt the class. They question everything you ask them to do and argue that you are picking on them. They make fun of you, throw things around the room and refuse to do the work, complaining that they can't see the point of it. They accuse you of teaching irrelevant topics, arrive late and leave early. When you discuss this with the beauty therapy tutor, she says that they are model learners in her class. What do you do?

If you've worked through the scenarios and have found it difficult coming to terms with the learner's behaviour or feel that you lack confidence in dealing with learners with challenging behaviour, then Eric Berne (2010) offers some great advice in his ground-breaking *Games People Play* in which he describes people who have either high or low confidence in themselves and high or low regard for others. Our interpretation of Berne's ideas can be found in Figure 3.4.

Berne's model can be summarised from the teacher's perspective as:

- **Low self-confidence** and **low regard for learner**: you can't be bothered offering comments about your learner's behaviour, resulting in a desperate situation which can descend into depression and loathing (of both yourself and your learner).
- **High self-confidence** but **low regard for learner**: criticisms about your learner's behaviour are intended as put-downs, resulting in frustration and anger with your learner and a feeling that they will never live up to your expectations of them.

- **Low self-confidence** but **high regard for learner**: you won't be critical of your learner's behaviour for fear of offending them, resulting in a lack of personal self-worth and a tendency to let the learner get away with what they want to.
- **High self-confidence** and **high regard for learner**: criticisms of your learner's behaviour are intended to develop them, resulting in a harmonious situation which will be characterised by constructive and cooperative relationships.

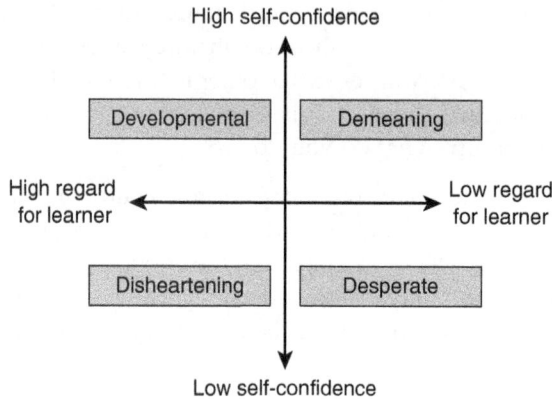

Figure 3.4   The 4D confidence–regard model

Berne argued that this model can be used to challenge your existing beliefs and values and to replace them with more constructive thoughts about yourself and others.

CONCLUSION

MANAGING BEHAVIOURS

Unfortunately, there are no hard and fast rules for dealing with the challenging behaviours that occur in the classroom. Here are 10 steps however for dealing with the behaviours that may disrupt your lessons. To help you remember these, we've used the acronym BEHAVIOURS as an aide-memoire:

Be friendly and supportive with your learners but know where the boundaries lie. It's very difficult to impose sanctions on someone who you have met on a social occasion. Treating individuals more favourably than others in the class will cause conflict.

Encourage learners not to be afraid of making mistakes. When learners lose confidence after making a mistake, they often turn to disruptive behaviour to compensate for this. Tell them that failing in something doesn't make them a failure.

Have a set of ground rules that are agreed with your learners, not imposed on them. Talk about the consequences of infringing or complying with ground rules. If your class feels a sense of ownership of the rules, they are less likely to infringe them.

Allow learners to work collaboratively not competitively. Competition can create tension which may result in conflict. Create a positive classroom environment where learners care about each other's ideas and can work together and learn from each other.

Vary teaching methods. Boredom is one of the main causes of disruption. By being familiar with each learner's learning style and implementing teaching methods to reach all of your class, you will reduce the risk of learners being bored.

Instil a love of learning. Lessons should be interesting and relevant to your learners' desired learning outcomes. Note that I say 'learners" learning outcomes, not 'your'. When learners feel that the content of the lesson is irrelevant, they quickly lose interest and start becoming disruptive.

Organise your learners into small groups when working on tasks. Mixing the members of small groups around will discourage cliques from forming and create a greater social bonding in the group. This will help prevent friction from developing in the group.

Understand what the cause of a learner's disruptive behaviour might be. You don't need the skills of a psychiatrist or a psychologist to do this, as a few simple questions might suffice. If the issue is more complex, then a referral to someone with more expertise in the issue may be necessary.

Rewards and threats are often not the best way of addressing the disruptions in the classroom. You may get some short-term gains by doing this but for long-term results you need to be thinking proactively rather than reactively.

Show patience, tolerance and understanding with your learners as they make their own choices in what and how they want to learn. Celebrate efforts, not just successes.

A TRUE STORY TO FINISH WITH: THE 12 DISRUPTERS AND THE LESSON IN THE MOUNT

The Mount is a secondary school that caters for children who have been excluded from mainstream education due to their challenging and often disruptive behaviour. The 12 pupils in the Year 12 class (often referred to as the impossibles) were being taught by their religious instruction teacher, Jessie, about the people who the scriptures claimed would be allowed to enter the kingdom of heaven. This was Jessie's last session with the class as she was moving to be a head of department at Golgotha Hill Academy School. As luck would have it, the school was being visited by Ofsted that week and Jessie's class was being observed.

As Jessie started talking about how blessed the poor were and how those that mourn would be comforted, and about the 'meek who would inherit the earth', Simone (aka the Sponge) turned to the two James' and said 'why does she never give us the National Office of Statistics for the number of poor people in the land?' 'Please be quiet', Andrea (aka the Sycophant) said out loud, 'she is the most amazing teacher in the school'. 'You can shut up', John (aka the Bully) shouted out, 'we all know how toady you were, carrying her iPad tablets on that field trip to Sinai'. 'Hey you lot, listen up', Peter (aka the Alpha Type) said, 'I think it's time we started planning next week's leaving supper with Jess'. 'I don't think she wants me there', said Thomas (aka the Doubter). 'I may not be well enough to go', James (aka the Prima Donna) said. 'I won't be there as I'm going on an Easter Egg hunt', Bart (aka the Procrastinator) chimed in. 'Well, I'll be there', said Dwayne (aka the Rock), 'you three are always coming up with weak-kneed excuses'. Matty (aka the Hermit) just sat there.

When Mr Pilate, the lead inspector, asked one of the pupils, Judy (aka the Shell), what she thought of Jessie's teaching, Judy told him: 'She's a nutcase, she keeps going on about how God-like her dad is. We all know he's just a chippy. Last week when she covered a class for our chemistry teacher she tried an experiment to turn water into wine!'

When Mr Pilate asked Jessie where her lesson plans were, what her learning outcomes were, what her differentiation and safeguarding strategies were, Jessie smiled nervously as she knew what fate awaited her.

We're not sure this is a true story, but why spoil a good story with the truth?

BIBLIOGRAPHY

Alderfer, C.P. (1972) *Existence, Relatedness, and Growth: Human Needs in Organizational Settings*. New York: Free Press.

Allen, J.G. and Fonagy, P. (2006) *Handbook of Mentalization-Based Treatment*. Chichester: John Wiley & Sons.

Bandler, R. and Grinder, J. (1990) *Frogs into Princes: Introduction to Neurolinguistic Programming*. Santa Barbara, CA: Eden Grove.

Bandura, A. (1977) *Social Learning Theory*. New York: General Learning Press.

Bateman, A. and Fonagy, P. (2006) *Mentalization-based Treatment for Borderline Personality Disorder: A Practical Guide*. Oxford: Oxford University Press.

Bateman, A. and Fonagy, P. (2016) *Mentalization-based Treatment for Personality Disorders*. Oxford: Oxford University Press.

Bates, B. (2015) *The Little Book of Big Coaching Theories*. London: Pearson.

Bates, B. (2017) *A Quick Guide to Special Needs and Disabilities*. London: Sage.

Beck, J.S. and Beck, A. (2010) *Cognitive Behavioural Therapy*. New York: Guilford Press.

Beever, S. (2009) *Happy Kids, Happy You: Using NLP to Bring Out the Best in Ourselves and the Child we Care for*. Carmarthen, Wales: Crown House Publishing.

Bennett, T. (2010) *The Behaviour Guru*. London: Continuum.

Bennett, T. (2016) *Developing Behaviour Management Content for Initial Teacher Training (ITT)*. London: Crown. Available at: https://assets.publishing.service.gov.uk/government/uploads/system/uploads/attachment_data/file/536889/Behaviour_Management_report_final__11_July_2016.pdf (accessed 10 December 2018).

Bentley, H., O'Hagan, O., Raff, A. and Bhatti, I. (2016) *How Safe are our Children?* London: NSPCC.

Berne, E. (2010) *Games People Play*. London: Penguin.

Bolton, G. (2010) *Reflective Practice: Writing and Personal Development*. London: Sage.

Brookfield, S. (1995) *Becoming a Critically Reflective Teacher*. San Francisco, CA: Jossey-Bass.

Canter, L. and Canter, M. (1992) *Assertive Discipline*. Los Angeles, CA: Canter and Associates.

Costa, A.L. and Kallick, B. (1993) Through the Lens of a Critical Friend. *Educational Leadership*, 51(2): 49–51.

Covey, S. (2004) *The 7 Habits of Highly Effective People*. London: Simon & Schuster.

Cowley, S. (2010) *Getting the Buggers to Behave*. London: Continuum.

Dahl, R. (1988) *Matilda*. London: Jonathan Cape.

Department for Education (DfE) (2015) *Protecting Children from Radicalisation: The Prevent Duty*. London: Gov.UK.

Department for Education (DfE) (2016) *Keeping Children Safe*. London: Gov.UK.

Descartes, R. (1966) *Philosophical Writings* (Anscombe, G. and Geach, P., trans. and ed.). London: Nelson.

Festinger, L. (1957) *A Theory of Cognitive Dissonance*. New York: Harper & Row.

Fitzgerald, S. (2013) *The CBT Workbook*. London: Hodder & Stoughton.

French, J.R.P. and Raven, B. (1959) 'The bases of social power'. In D. Cartwright (ed.) *Studies in Social Power*. Ann Arbor, MI: University of Michigan Press.

Gardner, H. (1993) *Multiple Intelligences: The Theory in Practice*. New York: Basic Books.

Golding, W. (1954) *Lord of the Flies*. London: Faber and Faber.

Goleman, D. (1996) *Emotional Intelligence: Why it Can Matter More Than IQ*. London: Bloomsbury.

Hainstock, E.G. (1997) *The Essential Montessori: An Introduction to the Woman, the Writings, the Method and the Movement*. New York: Plume.

Hanh, T.N. (2007) *Planting Seeds: Practicing Mindfulness with Children*. Berkeley, CA: Parallax Press.

Hare, R.D. (2003) *The Psychopathic Checklist* (revised 2nd edn). Toronto: Multi-Health Systems.

Harris, T. (1989) *I'm OK – You're OK*. London: Pan Books.

Hattie, J. (2012) *Visible Learning for Teachers*. Abingdon, Oxon: Routledge.

Hines, B. (1968) *A Kestrel for a Knave*. London: Penguin Books.

Kabat-Zinn, J. (1994) *Wherever You Go, There You Are*. New York: Hyperion.

Kohlberg, L. (1973) The Claim to Moral Adequacy of a Highest Stage of Moral Judgment. *Journal of Philosophy*, 70(18): 630–646.

Kohn, A. (1999) *Punished by Rewards*. New York: Mifflin Harcourt Publishing.

Leyden, S. (2013) *Supporting the Child of Exceptional Ability at Home and School*. New York: Routledge.

Locke, J. (1961) *An Essay Concerning Human Understanding*. London: Dent.

McGregor, D. (1985) *The Human Side of Enterprise*. New York: McGraw-Hill.

Machiavelli, N. (2004) *Penguin Great Ideas: The Prince*. London: Penguin.

Malone, J.C. (1990) *Theories of Learning: A Historical Approach*. CA: Wadsworth.

Maslow, A.H. (1993) *The Further Reaches of Human Nature*. London: Penguin.

Merton, R.K. (1948) The Self-fulfilling Prophecy. *The Antioch Review*, 8(2): 193–210.

Navia, L.E. (2007) *Socrates: A Life Examined*. New York: Prometheus Books.

Petty, G. (2009) *Teaching Today* (4th edn). Cheltenham: Nelson Thornes.

Piaget, J. (1957) *Construction of Reality in the Child*. London: Routledge & Kegan Paul.

Reece, I. and Walker, S. (2007) *Teaching, Training and Learning* (6th edn). Sunderland: Business Education Publishers.

Rogers, B. (2007) *Behaviour Management: A Whole School Approach*. London: Sage.

Rogers, B. (2015) *Classroom Behaviour: A Practical Guide to Effective Teaching, Behaviour Management and Colleague Support* (4th edn). London: Sage.

Ronson, J. (2011) *The Psychopath Test*. London: Picador.

Rousseau, J.-J. (1911) *Emile, or Education* (Foxley, B., trans.). London: Business Education Publishers.

Schön, D. (1983) *The Reflective Practitioner*. New York: Basic Books.

Schön, D. (1987) *Educating the Reflective Practitioner*. San Francisco, CA: Jossey-Bass.

Stallard, P. (2005) *A Clinician's Guide to Think Good – Feel Good: Using CBT with Children*. Chichester: Wiley.

Thomas, K.W. and Kilmann, R.H. (1974) *Thomas–Kilmann Conflict Mode Instrument*. New York: Xicom.

Vygotsky, L.S. (1978) *Mind in Society*. Cambridge, MA: Harvard University Press.

Watson, J.B. (1928) *The Ways of Behaviourism*. New York: Harper.

Weber, M. (2002) *Max Weber*. Abingdon, Oxon: Routledge.

Whitmore, J. (1998) *Coaching for Performance*. London: Nicholas Brealey.

APPENDIX 1: BOSTIN PERFORMANCE QUESTIONNAIRE (BPQ)

Look at each issue in the BPQ and indicate the level of importance (1 = Low; 7 = High) you attach to the issue. Then do the same for Performance (1 = Poor; 7 = Excellent).

The Bostin Performance Questionnaire

IMPORTANCE 1 2 3 4 5 6 7	ISSUE	PERFORMANCE 1 2 3 4 5 6 7
	Behaviour management policies that are implemented consistently and fairly throughout the organisation	
	Learners being carefully monitored in terms of their attendance and punctuality	
	Staff at all levels acting as exemplary role models in terms of their behaviour	
	Records of learners' disruptive behaviour being kept and monitored	
	Organisational leaders fostering a culture of mutual respect between all stakeholders in the organisation	
	All staff and learners being invited to contribute to developing policies and procedures on behaviour management	
	Activities are designed to stretch and challenge learners	
	Good use is made of teaching resources	

(Continued)

(Continued)

The Bostin Performance Questionnaire		
IMPORTANCE	ISSUE	PERFORMANCE
1 2 3 4 5 6 7		1 2 3 4 5 6 7
	Learning is constantly checked and summarised at the end of each session	
	Marking is meticulous and constructive feedback is given on time	
	Assessment of learners' work is fair and consistent	

Compare the scores for *Importance* and *Performance* on each of the issues. If the scores are the same or if there is a difference of +/– 1, there may not be a problem with that issue in the organisation. As the difference increases, the extent of the problem increases. If an *Importance* score far outweighs the *Performance* score on an issue, then the organisation clearly has to improve its approach to that issue. If a *Performance* score far outweighs the *Importance* score on an issue, then the organisation may be allocating too many resources to that issue.

APPENDIX 2: THE X–Y QUESTIONNAIRE

How would you describe your approach to teaching in the situations that follow?

It is important that you approach each question honestly. Do not give what you think is the desirable answer but respond by saying what you actually do.

There are 20 situations described below. Each situation has two possible responses (you may have others, but for the purpose of this exercise, we'll stick with the two suggested). You have 5 points to award to each pair of responses. If you favour A and would never contemplate B, then you would award 5 to A and nil to B (or vice versa). If you favour A but can see some merit in B, then scores allotted might be 4:1 or 3:2 or 2:3 or 1:4. The combination of scores is down to you but A + B in each case **must** equal 5.

| 1 | When it comes to setting tasks, I... | A | ...set tasks which do not necessarily have a right or wrong answer. | |
| | | B | ...only set tasks where there is one clear answer. | |

| 2 | When it comes to assessing learners' work, I... | A | ...assume total responsibility for this. | |
| | | B | ...allow learners some scope to assess their own work. | |

| 3 | When learners start a task, I... | A | ...give them clear instructions about what they should do. | |
| | | B | ...allow them to decide how they are going to approach the task. | |

| 4 | When it comes to deciding who will work with whom on group tasks, I... | A | ...allow learners to choose who they want to work with. | |
| | | B | ...always choose the groups. | |

| 5 | When it comes to learning materials, I... | A | ...always use the ones that I have designed. | |
| | | B | ...encourage learners to design their own. | |

| 6 | When it comes to lesson content, I... | A | ...am not afraid to vary from what is in the textbook. | |
| | | B | ...stick rigidly to what is in the textbook. | |

| 7 | When it comes to classroom discussion, I... | A | ...discourage learners from expressing opinions and feelings. | |
| | | B | ...openly welcome learners' strongly felt views on a subject. | |

| 8 | When it comes to lesson planning, I... | A | ...follow a fixed pattern that is determined by me. | |
| | | B | ...adopt a flexible approach and allow learners to determine the pattern of the lesson. | |

| 9 | In determining classroom rules, I... | A | ...allow the learners to decide what they feel are acceptable rules. | |
| | | B | ...dictate what is right or wrong. | |

| 10 | When it comes to setting learning objectives for a session, I... | A | ...tell learners what I want to achieve in the lesson. | |
| | | B | ...ask learners what they want to achieve in the lesson. | |

| 11 | If I think that a learner is making a mistake, I... | A | ...correct them immediately. | |
| | | B | ...allow them to find out for themselves where they are going wrong. | |

| 12 | In terms of my teaching, I... | A | ...regularly review and change my teaching methods. | |
| | | B | ...have tried and tested methods that I have used to good effect in the past. | |

| 13 | In terms of learner progress, I... | A | ...take every opportunity to review this with them. | |
| | | B | ...have set review times when we sit down together and discuss this. | |

| 14 | In terms of my teaching, I... | A | ...prefer to stand up in front of the class and teach the whole class. | |
| | | B | ...prefer organising the class into small groups. | |

| 15 | When it comes to asking questions, I... | A | ...encourage contributions from everyone in the class. | |
| | | B | ...avoid asking weaker learners for fear of embarrassing them. | |

| 16 | If any of my learners choose not to participate in the lesson, I... | A | ...leave them to it and concentrate on the rest of the class. | |
| | | B | ...think about ways that I can involve them in the lesson. | |

| 17 | In terms of learner performance, I... | A | ...have a set of rewards that I give for achieving good results. | |
| | | B | ...am more interested in the effort made than the actual results. | |

| 18 | In terms of dealing with disruptive learners, I... | A | ...try to find the reasons for their behaviour. | |
| | | B | ...have no hesitation in imposing sanctions on them. | |

| 19 | If I have a learner in my class who is regularly misbehaving, I... | A | ...ask other teachers if the learner is misbehaving in their class. | |
| | | B | ...keep quiet about it for fear of exposing any shortcomings that I have in classroom management. | |

| 20 | If I have a learner in my class who is being bullied by another learner, I... | A | ...refer the matter to the year head. | |
| | | B | ...talk to both the learner and the bully to find out what's happening. | |

Now transfer your scores for A and B onto the grid below.

1B			1A	
2A			2B	
3A			3B	
4B			4A	
5A			5B	
6B			6A	
7A			7B	
8A			8B	
9B			9A	
10A			10B	
11A			11B	
12B			12A	
13A			13B	
14A			14B	
15B			15A	
16A			16B	
17A			17B	
18B			18A	
19B			19A	
20A			20B	

X [ ]　　　　　　　　**Y** [ ]

APPENDIX 3: THE PROACTIVE–REACTIVE QUESTIONNAIRE

How would you, as a teacher, handle the interactions that follow?

It is important that you approach each question honestly. Do not give what you think is the desirable answer but respond by saying what you would do.

There are 20 situations described below. Each situation has two possible responses (you may have others, but for the purpose of this exercise, we'll stick with the two suggested). You have 5 points to award to each pair of responses. If you favour A and would never contemplate B, then you would award 5 to A and nil to B (or vice versa). If you favour A but can see some merit in B, then scores allotted might be 4:1 or 3:2 or 2:3 or 1:4. The combination of scores is down to you but A + B in each case **must** equal 5.

| 1 | If two of my learners had a personality conflict with each other, I would... | A | ...tell my learners that I felt they were equally responsible for any conflict and try to indicate how the rest of the class was being affected by their behaviour. | |
| | | B | ...not get involved and hope that they could sort it out themselves. | |

| 2 | If a learner of mine and I had engaged in a heated argument in the past, and I realised that they were ill at ease around me, I would... | A | ...avoid making matters worse by calling attention to their behaviour and let the whole thing drop. | |
| | | B | ...comment on their behaviour and ask them how they felt the argument had affected our relationship. | |

| 3 | If a learner of mine began to avoid me and act in an obedient but withdrawn manner, I would... | A | ...ask them to tell me what was on their mind. | |
| | | B | ...follow their lead and keep our contact on a 'business-only basis'. | |

| 4 | If I was asked a question by a learner on a subject about which I should be knowledgeable, but in reality I knew nothing about, I would... | A | ...try to steer the conversation in a different direction in case my credibility was called into question. | |
| | | B | ...confess my ignorance and assure the learner I would find out the answer. | |

| 5 | If a learner of mine was to tell me that my teaching methods were not effective, I would... | A | ...encourage them to elaborate on what faults they had observed and what changes they felt that I could make. | |
| | | B | ...ignore them because I know what's best for them. | |

| 6 | If a learner of mine wanted to do things that I felt were beyond their capabilities, I would... | A | ...not spell out my misgivings and let them handle things in their own way. | |
| | | B | ...tell them point blank about my misgivings. | |

| 7 | If I felt that a learner of mine was being unfair to other learners in the group, I would... | A | ...ask other learners how they perceived the situation and whether they felt the learner was behaving badly. | |
| | | B | ...wait for another learner to report the situation to me. | |

| 8 | If I was preoccupied with a personal matter and one of my learners told me that I was being irritable with them, I would... | A | ...tell them that I had a personal issue to deal with and that I might appear to be on edge for a while. | |
| | | B | ...listen to what they had to say but not try to explain my actions. | |

| 9 | If I heard some of my learners discussing an ugly rumour about another learner, which I know would hurt them if they found out and they asked me what I knew about it, I would... | A | ...plead ignorance of the matter and suggest that no one would believe such a rumour anyway. | |
| | | B | ...find out if there is any substance in the rumour and discuss the situation with the learner concerned. | |

| 10 | If one of my learners pointed out that I had a personality clash with another member of the teaching team and that it was affecting their studies, I would... | A | ...tell them that their comments were 'out of order' and discourage any further discussion on the matter. | |
| | | B | ...discuss it openly with them and find out how their studies were being affected. | |

| 11 | If my relationship with one of my learners was being damaged by frequent arguments on an issue of importance to both of us, I would... | A | ...be cautious in further discussions in case our relationship worsened. | |
| | | B | ...point to the effect that our disagreements were having on our relationship and suggest that we try and resolve our differences. | |

| 12 | If, during an assessment of one of my learner's performance, they suddenly suggest that we discuss my performance as well as theirs, I would... | A | ...forestall their comments by suggesting that others in the department are in a better position to assess my performance. | |
| | | B | ...welcome the opportunity to learn how they evaluated my performance and encourage future comments. | |

| 13 | If a learner of mine began to tell me of their hostile feelings towards one of my other learners, I would... | A | ...tell them to sort it out. | |
| | | B | ...call the two individuals together to discuss what the problem is. | |

| 14 | If I had reason to believe that an ugly rumour about me was being circulated in the class, I would... | A | ...avoid mentioning the issue and leave it to the group to tell me about it if they wanted to. | |
| | | B | ...risk putting learners on the spot by asking them to tell me what they knew about the rumour. | |

| 15 | If I disagreed strongly with another teacher's assessment of one of my learner's assignments, I would... | A | ...let the other teacher know that I could not accept their assessment and ask them to consider adjusting their grade. | |
| | | B | ...let them know that I have reservations about their assessment but accept their professional judgement. | |

| 16 | If it is not the school's policy for tutors to comment on draft assignments, but if one of my learners is worried about whether their assignment is satisfactory and asks me to 'have a look at it', I would... | A | ...raise it as an issue at the next Senior Management Team meeting to see if the policy can be changed. | |
| | | B | ...have a look at the assignment but ask the learner not to say anything to anyone about it. | |

| 17 | If a learner of mine was becoming irritated with me and their fellow learners, I would... | A | ...treat them with 'kid gloves' for a while on the presumption that they were having personal problems which were none of my business. | |
| | | B | ...try to talk it through with them and point out the effect that they were having on everyone. | |

| 18 | If I had a genuine dislike of one of my learners to the extent that it was affecting my work with them, I would... | A | ...say nothing to them and keep our relationship on a 'strictly professional' basis. | |
| | | B | ...get my feelings out in the open so that we can get on with our work. | |

| 19 | In discussing their performance with a learner who I felt would not take kindly to criticism, I would... | A | ...avoid emphasising their shortcomings so as not to injure their morale. | |
| | | B | ...focus on their shortcomings so as to help them improve. | |

| 20 | During a break in lessons, a learner tells the group a joke that I find offensive (the others laugh), I would... | A | ...tell them that I do not find jokes of that nature amusing. | |
| | | B | ...laugh, but without conviction, along with the rest of the group. | |

Now transfer your scores for A and B onto the grid below.

1A			1B	
2B			2A	
3A			3B	
4B			4A	
5A			5B	
6B			6A	
7A			7B	
8A			8B	
9B			9A	
10B			10A	
11B			11A	
12B			12A	
13A			13B	
14B			14A	
15A			15B	
16A			16B	
17B			17A	
18B			18A	
19B			19A	
20A			20B	

P   [＿＿＿＿＿]   **R**   [＿＿＿＿＿]

APPENDIX 4: SUGGESTIONS
FOR THE SCENARIOS

Scenario A: The acting head teacher (AHT) in this scenario told the boys that they had a collective responsibility for the crime. Some boys and girls looked horrified and some thought it was the comeuppance for a very unpopular boy. One of the AHT's mantras was 'We succeed and celebrate together and we fail and suffer together'. He said that all the boys would miss swimming the following week unless the culprit owned up before the day had ended. No one owned up and swimming was cancelled for the boys, much to their and their parents' disapproval and sense of injustice.

Just take a moment to consider the AHT's actions. Is the boy a victim of other's actions or a classic *procrastinator*? Do you agree with what the AHT did or would you suggest a different way of dealing with this instance of bad behaviour? Can you assume only one boy was involved – or indeed was there a third party involved? What would the implications for staffing be when girls are allowed to go swimming and boys forced to remain in school (remember, this is a very small school)? How would you use this example when you were compiling a school behaviour policy?

Scenario B: The inexperienced teacher in this scenario directed stern words at the whole class, pointing out that what had happened outside of the classroom should not be brought into it to disrupt the afternoon's planned learning. Attempts by some learners to continue the dispute were cut short and all learners were informed that no more time was to be wasted, and the lesson began. This worked for a short time, but an undercurrent remained, which developed by degrees into disorder to the point where the teacher was in danger of losing control.

This was a classic case of *rock v rock*. Greater experience would probably have led to the teacher understanding that, although it was important for the planned learning to commence as soon as possible, this sentiment was not shared by many members of the class; certainly not the two *rocks* and their followers, whose priorities were social rather than educational. Some time needed to be taken to resolve issues. In so doing, time would not be wasted; rather, social and moral issues could be addressed. With care, the situation could be exploited to develop learner skills in these areas and help them to actually resolve the conflict. Before doing so, it would be important to establish consistent ground rules for behaviour, which, when agreed, would allow the protagonists to state their cases, evidence to be supplied by witnesses, the rights and wrongs to be discussed and debated and a compromise verdict to be delivered.

Just take a moment to consider the teacher's actions. Maybe the teacher could have considered telling the class they will give this matter five minutes, as they have a lesson to engage with which is far more important than spending time on some dispute between two students. They could ask the protagonists what happened and make a judgement about the next step – obviously, this will be determined by the nature of the fall-out. Having shown them that they care about problems and upsets etc., the teacher could further take all the heat out of the situation by bringing the class back to their lesson. In doing so, they need to be decisive and begin the lesson. At the end, they could give them a quick reminder, perhaps holding back the *rocks* for a final 'whisper' in the ear, and wish everyone a pleasant rest of the day. It may not be a bad idea for the teacher to warn the next teacher or inform someone about the incident so that they are vigilant.

Scenario C: The teacher in this scenario informed the pupil that their outburst was unacceptable. When the pupil made it plain that he did not agree, the teacher attempted to promote the school's anti-racist stance but to no effect, and the comments of a small minority of pupils inflamed the situation which rapidly degenerated to the point where a senior member of staff had to be sent for.

This is clearly an example of the *shell* who shows no remorse for their behaviour. Teachers are often reluctant to refer badly behaved pupils to senior members of staff, fearing that they will be seen to be failing in the eyes of their seniors and their pupils. However, some issues are too important not to bring to the attention of senior staff; racism is such an issue. In fairness to the pupil, they could have been given an opportunity to apologise and demonstrate some contrition. If unwilling to do so then it would be wholly appropriate for the teacher to refer the pupil to a senior member of staff. The influence that the pupil in question may have on other members of the class at the time needs to be cauterised. Removing them from the class reduces their influence on others, takes the heat out of the situation and allows the teacher to deal with issues raised in a calm and measured manner with the other pupils in line with school policy. There is nothing wrong with instigating the intervention of a senior member of staff, provided that the teacher is not putting themselves in a position where this is seen by pupils and senior staff to be a sign of weakness.

Just take a moment to consider the teacher's actions. Maybe the teacher could stop what they are doing and deal with what has just happened/been said. They could then get the class to distance themselves from the remark by saying something like, 'I'm sure you're as shocked as I am at hearing what has just been said'. If the response from the class is one of disagreement with the *shell*'s comments, then the teacher should try to see if they can get them to say that it was racist and agree that they don't accept any form of racism. Doubtless, there is a school policy about such occurrences so apply it. Having isolated the pupil, tell them what will happen next and keep the rest of the class as one by confirming what was unacceptable and praising them for their universal disgust.

Scenario D: The teacher concerned was anxious to carry on with their teaching and provided the pupil with a quick explanation of what had been covered so far in the lesson. However, the pupil was uncooperative and engaged in attention-seeking behaviour, to which the teacher responded. This interrupted the flow of the lesson as she became flustered and led to a number of pupils losing focus.

This isn't an easy situation to deal with. The pupil may just be exhibiting signs of the *movie star*, craving attention, or it may be something more serious like a case of bullying or abuse. In an ideal world, it would have been great for the teacher to have carried on when teaching was going so well. However, this is a situation that cannot be ignored. The teacher could have set pupils a task for a short period of time in order to be able to talk quietly with the pupil and try to ascertain why they are behaving as they are. Their response will then depend on what is ascertained. If the pupil is forthcoming, it should be possible to reassure them that support will be provided at the earliest opportunity (later in the lesson or at breaktime), allowing the teacher time to complete what is necessary with the rest of the class. If they remain unforthcoming or uncooperative, she could continue explaining learning to the class, ignoring attention-seeking behaviour rather than confronting it. When the class is working on the planned task, the teacher can refocus on attempting to resolve the situation.

Just take a moment to consider the teacher's actions. If, having tried all the strategies they have used before, there is no improvement in the pupil's behaviour, do you think that the teacher has no alternative but to send for the deputy head teacher and request the pupil is removed from their lesson? Do you think that all the other members of class should suffer from the actions of one, whatever (s)he has been experiencing before school? If you go along with that action, then, having done that, it is important that the teacher speaks to the deputy head teacher later to voice their concerns about the pupil's (suspected) home circumstances so that they can be investigated further. The pupil might need counselling or require an opportunity to divulge something or just need a shoulder to cry on. Is this something that you would be prepared to do?

Scenario E: The teacher in this scenario was aware of being held to account by senior members of staff who set targets for pupil achievement at half-termly pupil progress meetings. The teacher attempted to bring these pupils on-side through a set of rewards for achievement and behaviour. This was partially successful; some pupils responded well, however it had little impact on others, and by the end of the year there was a small hardcore of demotivated and, in some cases, poorly behaved pupils.

The teacher in this scenario didn't want to turn their pupils into *results merchants*, who have little concern for their long-term development. It is important therefore that they try to establish why pupils are becoming demotivated. Just because increased academic intensity appears to be the catalyst for behaviour changes, its impact on these pupils might be different. Different remedies may therefore be appropriate for individual pupils. Some pupils could be responding adversely to the increased pressure on them to succeed; the more they are helped, the more they fear failure. Some may resent the narrowing of the curriculum; in focusing on 'important' subjects, they may be spending less time on subjects they enjoy or have more success in. It could even be that, in attempting to 'crank up' results, unrealistic demands are being placed on one or two pupils. Targets for pupils using data relating to their prior achievement may be invalidated due to subsequent changes in a pupil's life – such as a health issue or a family bereavement – which would render projections unsound.

Just take a moment to consider the teacher's actions. It may be necessary for the teacher to rethink their strategies. It is very easy to solve a problem whilst creating another one. Remember the adage that, in instances like this, one size never fits all. Maybe they need to ask colleagues for advice. All members of a teacher's class are important, none more or less than others, so they must reflect on the successes and failings of what they have planned and are delivering. Sometimes, we blame others for our mistakes and it takes a strong person to say, 'I haven't got this quite right' or 'How does this situation I've created sound to you?'. If the teacher does nothing, they are sacrificing those pupils whose progress has stalled. They are also jeopardising the progress of all, since the deteriorating behaviour of some and the poor engagement of others will undoubtedly affect those whose progress is accelerating at the moment.

Scenario F: The teacher in this scenario saw the pupil in question as a threat. They were a strong personality and appeared to be popular with a number of members of the class. The teacher therefore attempted to eclipse the pupil, by ensuring in words and actions that their influence on members of the class was stronger. In effect, the teacher instigated a popularity contest in which they had little chance of coming out on top, as their opponent's influence extended outside of the classroom and school. Over the course of the next few weeks, there was little or no improvement in the situation; rather, the teacher felt relationships with the class were becoming more fraught.

Just take a moment to consider the teacher's actions. Is the teacher dealing with the class *bully* who likes to intimidate or an *alpha type* who likes to be leader of the pack? In attempting to deal with this situation, it's important that the teacher tries to understand the underlying causes of the pupil's behaviour in order to attempt to fashion an appropriate response. It could also be worth them evaluating why some pupils are being influenced by Charlie. Is it anything to do with how they are being taught, the teacher's attitude to the pupil concerned, or are they a stronger character, able to exert more influence, or do they have more to offer other pupils? If it can be established that the deteriorating behaviour of other pupils is due to the influence of this pupil, then it is important to discover whether this is because of undue pressure being brought to bear on them, or the result of bullying. If this is the case, then the school's policy on bullying needs to be followed. When dealing with the pupil, the teacher needs to remain objective and not become hostile to them or engage in a competition as the teacher in the scenario did; sanctions are probably inevitable on occasions, but actions taken as a result of inappropriate behaviour should always be seen to be fair, in proportion to any offence and never personal.

A further, and more important, consideration is why is Charlie now demotivated? It sounds as if he was motivated once, so the teacher needs to find out what has happened. One approach could be to talk to him about his attitude, his work rate and his poor behaviour. Maybe the teacher could ask one of Charlie's friends? Is there a brother or sister in the school? Arrange a meeting with Charlie's parents – the school policy will determine how this is done and who would be at the meeting. Whatever approach is adopted, the teacher needs to collect all of the evidence, including what efforts they have put into improving the situation. So much could be learned from what happens in this situation.

Scenario G: The teacher in this scenario saw the justice of the case and modified the distribution of rewards to ensure fairness. This failed to satisfy some of the members of the target group, whose behaviour subsequently slipped.

The system of rewards being employed rewarded some, but not all, individuals. Competition is all well and good when you are the beneficiary; it is not so appealing when the rewards are passing you by. The rewards system could have been designed to spread the benefits as widely as possible. It could be that pupils earn points/merits that are pooled and then periodically there is a class reward if they reach or exceed a certain total. Similarly, there could be teams/houses/groups within the class and points/merits are earned for these: the winning group then receives a reward. Such a system allows all pupils to buy into it; those pupils who, under the other system, thought that they were being unjustly overlooked have a vested interest in the success of other pupils.

Just take a moment to consider the teacher's actions. Is this particular teacher just dealing with the symptoms and not the cause of the problem? Maybe the teacher needs to draw their concern to the attention of senior leaders – pointing out that the policy relating to rewards needs tweaking. People in school forget that if a positive behaviour policy is only about going upwards, it is flawed for several reasons. Just ask a steeplejack and they will tell you that what goes up can also go down! It might be a steady climb but a swift fall. More mountaineers are killed when descending, not ascending. So, if the school's policy rewards climbers, especially those who are struggling, and demotivates those who are showing strength and commitment, then it needs revising.

Scenario H: In this scenario, the teacher stopped the lesson and students were directed to return to their original seats/work stations and asked about the missing knife. The teacher reminded the students that anyone with information must disclose it but, with nothing forthcoming, told the class that she would have to call the technician to do a search of the room, and also the Senior Leadership Team who would attend, enquire, search bags and then decide on the next course of action. Students would not be allowed to leave the room and the next class would not be able to enter. The knife was found behind a radiator whereupon a boy admitted he had hidden it for a joke. One of the deputy head teachers took the boy to the head teacher who informed his parents and asked them to attend an immediate meeting to discuss the situation and determine punishment. The teacher was instructed to re-house the knife block in a secure position.

Just take a moment to consider the teacher's actions. Do you agree or would you suggest a different way of dealing with this instance of bad behaviour? Can you be certain that the boy had hidden the knife as a joke or was he intending to return later to steal the knife. How would you use this example when you were compiling a school behaviour policy?

Scenario I: The teacher listened carefully and asked the girl to confirm what she had said. Next, they made it clear to the girl that the matter would be passed on to the head of year and form teacher who would take up the matter and, at some point, want to speak to the girl. The teacher then reported the disclosure to the head of year and the form teacher. They said the teacher had acted correctly and the matter was now out of their hands. They would speak with the *whistle-blower* (WB) that evening and deal with the matter the following day.

WB was interviewed that evening (without any students realising) with the two members of staff present. The following day, the girl who had allegedly taken the photographs was also interviewed by the same members of staff. She denied taking photographs and told the interviewers that the boarders resented the day students – this was an issue that the staff were aware of. She voluntarily offered up her phone and there were no photographs of other girls on it. The identity of WB was not given. Senior staff considered the matter and decided:

- to inform the girl's parents about the incident with a full explanation of their actions in scrutinising her phone and, that being satisfied she had done no wrong, she was the victim of mischief
- to speak to WB again to inform her there were no photographs of girls in the changing room on the phone and to ascertain her reason for disclosing the issue which was deemed to be untrue
- to re-visit the school rules about mobile phones vis-à-vis safeguarding and make a recommendation to the deputy head teacher
- to ask staff to keep an eye on both girls.

Just take a moment to consider the teacher's actions. It appears that the staff used their knowledge about the past behaviours of the girls and their somewhat fractious relationship. Do you think the matter was handled satisfactorily, or was something missed or missing in the way it was concluded?

Scenario J: This a classic clash of the *alpha types*. In the animal world, the alpha males will fight to the death to see who rules the herd. As much as you would maybe like to lock them in a room together and see who emerges victorious, we're not sure this would solve the problem. In this case, the class teacher set them a really challenging task of analysing the effectiveness of a police investigation of a murder crime. As a pair, they would be expected to present their findings to the rest of the class. The teacher made it clear that they would be assessed as a pair and not as individuals. In this way, they were encouraging cooperation rather than competition.

Just take a moment to consider the teacher's actions. If you like what they did and decide to follow this approach, don't be too prescriptive in how you want learners to tackle the task but do describe how you will assess the way they have collaborated, produced and presented the task. You could also involve the rest of the class by encouraging them to ask questions of the two individuals about how they worked together and make comments about their style.

Scenario K: In this instance, the teacher decided that Ellen had to be taken down a peg or three. They set the class a task to collect an array of common garden weeds and make an attractive hanging basket display out of them. They told the group that they had one hour to complete the task. The names of the weeds to be collected and used were written down on pieces of paper and handed to each of the students. The teacher told the group that this was being done randomly but made sure that Ellen's list contained weeds that were not easy to find or were unattractive specimens. The inevitable happened and Ellen's pathetic effort made her something of a laughing stock with the rest of the class.

Just take a moment to consider the teacher's actions. This is a classic case of the *superstar*. Telling Ellen to shut up or waiting until one of the members of the group does this for you may solve the problem but may not do a lot for Ellen's self-esteem. Her boasting may be masking her lack of confidence and we're not sure that embarrassing her in the way that her teacher did was the right thing to do, and may even have been an abuse of her position. What do you think?

Scenario L: In this situation, the instructor tried role reversal. They got each of the *jokers* (separately) to do a demonstration and made sure that they interrupted them frequently with annoying comments and jokes: in other words, the teacher gave them a taste of their own medicine. If this doesn't work, we suggest a simpler approach – tell the *jokers* that they are not helping you, their group, nor themselves and consider warning them that you will have to speak to their employers; also warn them that you may have to have them removed from the sessions. Working on a building site can be a very challenging situation for a young person. There is almost a rite of passage that new recruits have to be the butt of humour rather than the joker. We're not saying that we agree with this; it is however very much the case. Taking on other, more experienced building workers, therefore, may not be good tactics and it may be much better to be seen and not heard. Impress on the class *jokers* that they may wish to tone down their joking around.

Just take a moment to consider the instructor's actions. What do you think about giving disruptive learners a taste of their own medicine? Is contacting their employer a bit heavy-handed? How would you handle this situation?

Scenario M: This can be very frustrating for any teacher. Some things are unacceptable (such as arriving late and leaving early) but these may be symptoms of something being very wrong. How does everyone else in the class behave? Do they engage? Are they making progress? You always have to step outside the situation and see it as an observer. You may begin to question your own teaching ability. Quite rightly so! If the learners are not disrupters by nature then you need to look at your course content or your teaching approach to find out why they are not engaging with your lessons. In this situation, the teacher asked the beauty therapy tutor to sit in on one of their sessions and observe how it went; then got feedback from her. They also sat in on one of her sessions. Needless to say, on both occasions there was a marked improvement in the disrupters' behaviour.

Just take a moment to consider the teacher's actions. If you need support, you have to seek it. It can be painful getting criticised, but it's more painful floundering and failing. Asking a colleague to observe your session is a good idea, but using a colleague who also teaches the class may not be the best solution as the learners are less likely to be disruptive when they are present. The section on the critical friend may be useful here.

INDEX

NOTE: page numbers in *italic type* refer to figures.